Rudolph August Witthaus

A Laboratory Guide in Urinalysis and Toxicology

Rudolph August Witthaus

A Laboratory Guide in Urinalysis and Toxicology

ISBN/EAN: 9783742816849

Manufactured in Europe, USA, Canada, Australia, Japa

Cover: Foto ©Lupo / pixelio.de

Manufactured and distributed by brebook publishing software (www.brebook.com)

Rudolph August Witthaus

A Laboratory Guide in Urinalysis and Toxicology

A LABORATORY GUIDE

IN

URINALYSIS AND TOXICOLOGY

BY

R. A. WITTHAUS, A.M., M.D.

PROFESSOR OF CHEMISTRY, PHYSICS, AND TOXICOLOGY IN THE MED. DEPT. CORNELL
UNIVERSITY; PROFESSOR OF CHEMISTRY AND TOXICOLOGY IN THE MED. DEPT.
UNIVERSITY OF VERMONT; MEMBER OF THE AMERICAN CHEMICAL SOCIETY,
AND OF THE CHEMICAL SOCIETIES OF PARIS AND BERLIN, ETC.

NEW YORK
WILLIAM WOOD & COMPANY
1898

CONTENTS.

	PAGE.
GENERAL RULES	1
METRIC WEIGHTS AND MEASURES	4
MANIPULATION AND ANALYTICAL REACTIONS	5
Bunsen flame	5
Solution	6
Filtration	6
Precipitation	8
Reaction	9
REACTIONS OF ACID RESIDUES	10
Chlorids	10
Hydrochloric acid	10
Bromids	11
Iodids	11
Cyanids	12
Nitrates	13
Nitric acid	13
Chlorates	14
Acetates	14
Oxids	14
Sulfids	14
Sulfites	15
Sulfates	15
Sulfuric acid	15
Thiosulfates	16
Carbonates	16
Oxalates	17
Tartrates	17
Phosphates	18
Arsenates	18
Antimonates	19
Borates	19
Citrates	20
Summary	21

CONTENTS.

	PAGE.
ACIDIC ELEMENTS GROUPED FOR ANALYSIS	22
REACTIONS OF BASES	22
Manganese	24
Iron	24
Aluminium	25
Lead	25
Bismuth	26
Tin	27
Lithium	27
Sodium	28
Potassium	28
Ammonium	29
Silver	29
Calcium	29
Barium	30
Magnesium	30
Zinc	31
Copper	31
Mercury	32
Summary	34
BASES GROUPED FOR ANALYSIS	35
EXAMINATION OF MIXTURES OF SALTS	37
QUALITATIVE ANALYSIS OF URINE	46
Physical Characters	46
Quantity	46
Color	46
Odor	46
Reaction	47
Specific gravity	47
Chemical Characters, Composition	49
Urea	49
Uric acid	50
Albumin	50
Paraglobulin	53
Mucin	53
Peptone	53
Glucose	54
Blood	58
Bile	59

CONTENTS.

	PAGE.
QUANTITATIVE ANALYSIS OF URINE	62
Reaction	62
Chlorids	65
Phosphates	66
Sulfates	68
Urea	69
Uric acid	71
Albumin	72
Glucose	73
URINARY DEPOSITS	75
Unorganized deposits	75
Organized deposits	78
QUALITATIVE ANALYSIS OF URINARY CALCULI	82
DETECTION OF POISONS	84
Volatile Poisons	84
Phosphorus	85
Hydrocyanic acid	87
Alcohol	87
Chloroform	88
Chloral	88
Phenol	89
MINERAL POISONS	90
Mineral Acids and Alkalies	90
Metallic Poisons	91
Arsenic	94
Antimony	99
Bismuth	100
Copper	101
Lead	101
Mercury	101
Barium	101
Zinc	101
VEGETABLE POISONS	102
General Reactions	104
Morphin	105
Meconic acid	106
Strychnin	106

LABORATORY GUIDE.

GENERAL RULES FOR WORKING.

1. The student's table and shelves with the bottles and apparatus must be kept clean.
2. There is a place for everything, into which it must be put *immediately* after use.
3. The reagent bottles must be kept on their shelves with labels outward, and in the following order from the gas fixture—

Middle Shelf.

HCl—Hydrogen chlorid—Hydrochloric acid.
H_2S— " sulfid.
H_2SO_4 " sulfate—Sulfuric acid.
HNO_3— " nitrate—Nitric acid.
$H(C_2H_3O_2)$—Hydrogen acetate—Acetic acid.
Fe_2Cl_6—Ferric chlorid.
$FeSO_4$—Ferrous sulfate.
HNa_2PO_4—Disodic phosphate.
KHO—Potassium hydroxid.
$K_4[Fe(CN)_6]$—Potassium ferro-cyanid.
$AgNO_3$—Silver nitrate.
NH_4HO—Ammonium hydroxid.

Bottom Shelf.

NH_4Cl—Ammonium chlorid.
NH_4HS— " hydrosulfid.
$(NH_4)_2CO_3$— " carbonate.
$CaCl_2$—Calcium chlorid.
$BaCl_2$—Barium chlorid.
$CuSO_4$—Cupric sulfate.
Indigo solution.
Fehling's solution.
Litmus papers.

GENERAL RULES FOR WORKING.

Top Shelf (one bottle to four students).

CaH_2O_2—Calcium hydroxid.
NaClO—Sodium hypochlorite.
Phenolphthalein solution.
Guaiacum tincture.
Ozonic ether.
Bottles containing specimens.
MnO_2—Manganese dioxid   (solid).
NaCl—Sodium chlorid   "
Na_2CO_3—Sodium carbonate   "
$HKSO_4$—Monopotassic sulfate   "
Uric acid.

4. Other reagents will be found and used at the instructor's table, but may not be removed.

5. Reagent bottles will be filled, and supplies obtained, at the assistant's table.

6. All apparatus issued to the students must be kept, when not in use, in the drawer or closet of the desk.

7. In replenishing reagent bottles from stock, fill them only half-full.

8. If the reagent in any bottle become cloudy, filter it.

9. Take up the reagent bottle by its body, thumb on one side of label, fingers on the opposite; and while pouring or dropping from the bottle keep the label side up. *Do not lay the stopper of the bottle upon the table.* Remove it from the bottle by grasping it between the little and ring fingers of the left hand, and hold it there, pointing outward from the back of the hand, until replaced in the bottle.

10. In liquid tests, use about two cent. of the liquid to be tested in a test-tube; not more unless so directed.

11. Add the reagent in small quantity at first, and stop when the desired end is attained.

12. Prevent the last drop adhering to the lip of the bottle from flowing down its side, by catching it upon the stopper or upon the *clean* lip of the test-tube.

13. A separate portion of the original substance or liquid is to be used for each test, except when otherwise directed.

14. Before trying a reaction, read the description through, and then follow the directions literally. *Should the result not be that described, ask for an explanation.*

15. Wash apparatus as soon as possible after using, *while still wet*, then two or three rinsings with a small quantity of clean water will suffice. If not clean, use 2-3 drops HCl with 2-3 cent. water; or KHO, and even a probang or brush if necessary. Set aside in a clean place to drain.

16. Do not scratch the inside of any glass vessel with wire or a broken glass rod.

17. Let each piece of apparatus be clean before being put into its place, and let everything be in its place before you leave.

Students are required to take notes, consult manuals, and construct equations representing the simpler chemical reactions.

ABBREVIATIONS.

The following abbreviations are used in the text, and will be found convenient by the student in taking notes:

ppt. = precipitate	pt.—pts. = part—parts
pptn. = precipitation	dil. = dilute

METRIC WEIGHTS AND MEASURES.   4

sol. = soluble
insol. = insoluble
soln. = solution
cc. = cubic centimetre
L. = litre
c. p. = chemically pure

cent. = centimetres
gtt. = drops
sp. gr. = specific gravity
con. = concentrated
gm. = gram

The formula *of the reagent* always applies to its solution, except where otherwise specified.

Metric weights and measures, and the centigrade thermometric scale, are used throughout.

One decimetre.

1 millimetre	= 0.001 metre	= 0.0394 inch.
1 centimetre	= 0.01 "	= 0.3937 "
1 decimetre	= 0.1 "	= 3.9371 inches.
1 METRE		= 39.3708 "
1 decametre	= 10 metres	= 32.8089 feet.
1 hectometre	= 100 "	= 328.089 "
1 kilometre	= 1000 "	= 0.6214 mile.

1 millilitre	=	1 cc.	= 0.001 litre	= 16.232 minims.
1 centilitre	=	10 "	= 0.01 "	= 2.705 fluid drachms.
1 decilitre	=	100 "	= 0.1 "	= 3.384 " ounces.
1 LITRE		= 1000 "		= 1.057 quarts.
1 decalitre			= 10 litres	= 2.642 gallons.
1 hectolitre			= 100 "	= 26.418 "
1 kilolitre			= 1000 "	= 264.18 "

1 milligram	= 0.001 gram	=	0 015 grain Troy.
1 centigram	= 0.01 "	=	0.154 " "
1 decigram	= 0.1 "	=	1.543 grains Troy.
1 GRAM		=	15.432 " "
1 decagram	= 10 grams	=	154.324 " "
1 hectogram	= 100 "	=	0.268 lb. Troy.
1 kilogram	= 1000 "	=	2.679 lbs. "
"	" "	=	2.205 " Avdp.

MANIPULATION AND ANALYTICAL REACTIONS.

Bunsen Flame.

18. Bunsen's burner is so constructed that street-gas is mixed with air to insure complete oxidation of the carbon without the intermediate or luminous stage.

To light the burner, close the air openings, a, Fig. 1, turn on the gas full, wait a second or two, then light at b, turn down the flame to about six cent. high, and open the air-holes gradually until the luminous part of the flame just disappears. If a smaller flame be desired, close the air-holes, reduce the flame, and then admit enough air to render the flame colorless. A proper adjustment of air and gas will prevent the burner becoming lit below at the jet c. If this should happen it will be recognized by a peculiar odor and change in the shape and color of the flame. The gas must be turned off and the burner cooled before relighting.

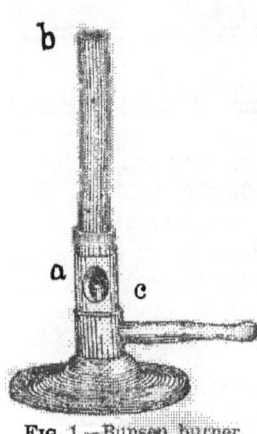

FIG. 1.—Bunsen burner.

19. While heating a liquid in a test-tube, hold the tube inclined, point it away from the face, and keep the contents constantly agitated by shaking or turning. In no case should the flame come in contact with a glass vessel above the level of the liquid within.

SOLUTION—FILTRATION.

Solution.

20. Place 10 cc. water in a small beaker, add about one gram solid NaCl, agitate: the salt disappears, dissolving completely in the water. Now add some PbCrO$_4$, agitate: this compound does not dissolve, but remains suspended in the liquid. If allowed to stand several hours, the particles of chromate will fall to the bottom, and the clear liquid might be poured off or **decanted**. Complete separation may be obtained immediately by the use of a filter.

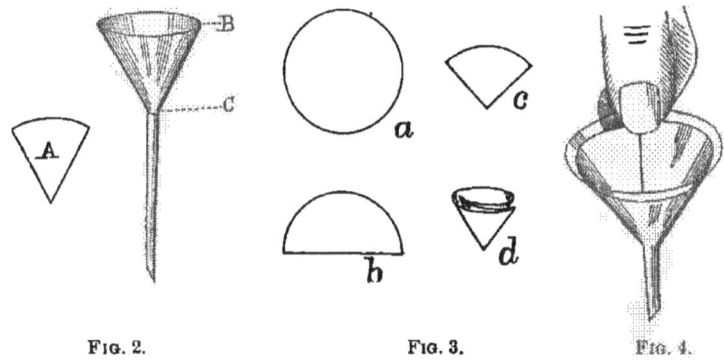

Fig. 2.   Fig. 3.   Fig. 4.

Filtration.

21. The apparatus required for this purpose consists of a funnel and support for the same, a vessel to receive the *filtrate* (*i.e.*, the liquid which passes through the filter), a wash-bottle, stirring-rod, and *filters*.

The funnel (Fig. 2) should be selected by testing with a piece of cardboard cut with an angle of 60° (A, Fig. 2), which should exactly fit it; and it should have the point of the stem ground off at an angle.

The filters are discs of porous paper manufactured for the purpose (filter paper). The diameter of the disc selected should be somewhat less than twice the length of the sloping side of the funnel from rim to shoulder (B–C, Fig. 2). The filter must not project above the rim of the funnel.

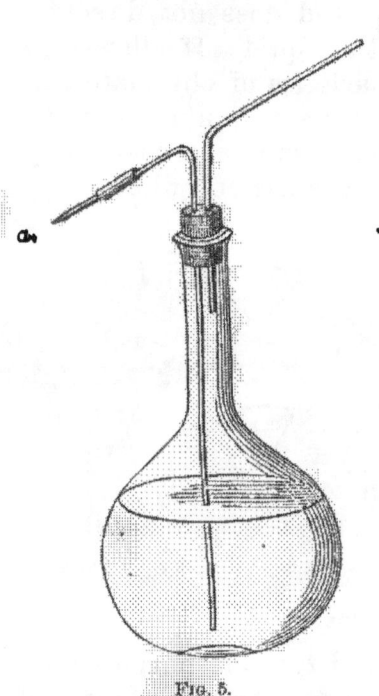

Fig. 5.

22. Take a filter (*a*, Fig. 3) of suitable size and fold it across a diameter (*b*, Fig. 3), fold it again over a radius at right angles to the first diameter (*c*, Fig. 3), open the paper out into a conical bag by separating one thickness of the paper from the other three (*d*, Fig. 3). The filter is then adjusted in the funnel and pressed against its side with the *dry finger* until it fits closely. Now, holding the filter and funnel so that the nail of the forefinger is pressed against the upper end of one of the folds (Fig. 4), moisten the paper by directing upon it a jet of water from the orifice *a* of the wash-bottle (Fig. 5), produced by blowing gently into the tube *b*.

23. Support the funnel containing the wetted filter over the vessel destined to receive the filtrate (if a flask or test-tube be used for this purpose, no other support is needed), and pour the liquid to be filtered into the filter, allowing it to flow along the stirring-

rod, held as shown in Fig. 6, in successive portions until it has passed through; never, however, adding liquid in greater quantity than to within two to three millimetres of the edge of the filter.

24. Remove the sediment to the filter by directing a jet of water from the wash-bottle upward into the beaker. Detach adhering particles by rubbing with a small bit of rubber tubing slipped on the end of a stirring rod.

25. After all the solid matter has been transferred to the filter, it must be washed until free from the soluble salt.

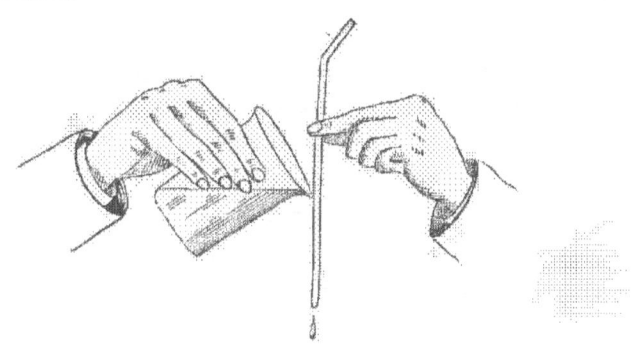

Fig 6.

Direct a gentle stream from the wash-bottle on the sediment in the filter, avoiding any loss by spurting or overflowing. Repeat after each washing has run completely through, and until the filtrate has no taste or does not respond to a suitable reagent.

Precipitation.

26. While the sediment is being washed, the filtrate may be tested for NaCl. Take two cent. water in a test-tube, add a few drops of the filtrate and a drop or two of $AgNO_3$: a copious white precipitate results from the chemical union of the chlorin of NaCl and silver of $AgNO_3$:

$$NaCl + AgNO_3 = AgCl + NaNO_3.$$

AgCl is insoluble in water, hence the ppt.; $NaNO_3$ is soluble, therefore remains in solution.*

Divide the contents of the test-tube, add to one part NH_4HO and agitate: the ppt. dissolves. Add to the other HNO_3: the ppt. does not dissolve.

Precipitation is complete when further additions of the reagent will not increase the precipitate.

27. Precipitates vary from a faintly visible cloud to a dense mass. They may be crystalline, amorphous, or curdy (coagulum); may fall to the bottom of the vessel, float on the surface, or be disseminated throughout the liquid menstruum.

Reaction.

28. Compounds are either **acid**, **alkaline**, or **neutral**, a property determined by their action on certain coloring matters, as litmus, turmeric, or phenolphthalein, called **indicators**.

29. Place 10 cc. water in a porcelain capsule, add a piece of blue and a piece of red litmus paper: there is no change, the water is neutral. Add to the water a few drops NH_4HO. stir with stirring-rod: both papers are blue, the reaction is alkaline. Add HCl drop by drop until the papers turn red: the acid is then in excess, and the reaction is acid.

30. In dark-colored solutions the bits of paper

* A **Table of Solubilities** will be found on pages 108, 109. By reference to this table the student will learn what substances may or cannot be present in solutions under examination.

should be removed from the solutions with a stirring-rod, or they may be drawn up the side of the capsule, for more careful examination.

31. In very weak solutions the change takes place slowly, and it is necessary to allow the test-papers to remain a minute or more before recording the reaction.

32. To neutralize an acid solution use NH_4HO; or if alkaline, use HCl, except when otherwise directed.

REACTIONS OF THE MORE COMMON ACID RESIDUES.

Chlorids. (M)'Cl. Use HCl.

33. Add 5 gtt. HCl to 5 cc. H_2O in a capsule, neutralize with KHO, divide the liquid in two test-tubes, and apply tests §§ 34 and 35, adding the reagent drop by drop.

34. $AgNO_3$ gives a white ppt. (AgCl) which darkens on exposure to sunlight. Divide ppt. in two test tubes, add to one NH_4HO and agitate; the ppt. dissolves (sol. in NH_4HO). To the other add HNO_3; the ppt. does not dissolve (insol. in HNO_3). KCN and $Na_2S_2O_3$ will also dissolve the ppt.

35. $Hg_2(NO_3)_2$ gives a white ppt. (Hg_2Cl_2) which turns black on the addition of NH_4HO.

(See also § 44.)

Hydrochloric Acid. HCl.

36. The free acid responds to the tests given above for chlorids, has a strong acid reaction, and when heated with powdered black oxid of manganese (MnO_2) gives off chlorin; recognizable by its odor, its yellow color, and by its power of turning paper containing starch and potassium iodid blue.

Bromids. (M)'Br. Use KBr.

37. AgNO₃ gives a yellowish-white ppt. (AgBr), sparingly soluble in NH₄HO and insoluble in HNO₃.

38. Chlorin water causes the solution to turn yellow. This, shaken with 2-3 drops of carbon bisulfid, will give a brown-red color to the reagent, which sinks to the bottom of the tube.

Iodids. (M)'I. Use KI.

39. AgNO₃ gives a yellowish ppt. (AgI), insoluble in NH₄HO and in HNO₃.

40. Chlorin water colors the liquid yellow, and gives a violet color to carbon bisulfid, with which it is agitated. If added to starch paste: turns black or purple.

41. CuSO₄. Add to an iodid a few drops of a mixture of one part CuSO₄ and two parts FeSO₄, warm: a white ppt.

42. HgCl₂ gives a scarlet ppt. (HgI₂), sol. in excess of either iodid or reagent.

43. Pb(C₂H₃O₂)₂ gives a yellow ppt. (PbI₂). (Chlorids and bromids give a white ppt.)

Dry Test for Cl, Br, and I.

44. Mix the solid substance (chlorid, bromid, or iodid) with a mixture of equal parts of HKSO₄ and MnO₂, place in the bottom of a closed matrass, a, Fig. 7, using a narrow paper shovel; attach a piece of moistened blue litmus paper in the mouth of the matrass, b, and apply heat to the closed end. Note the color and odor of the gas

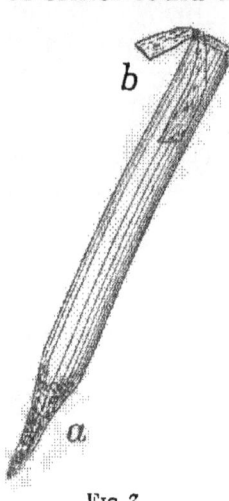

Fig. 7.

CYANIDS. 12

evolved, its action on the litmus, and condensation on the sides of the tube:

	Gas.	Odor.	Litmus.	Condensation.
Cl	green	characteristic	bleaches	none*
Br	red-brown	pungent	bleaches	brown drops
I	violet	peculiar	reddens	dark scales

Cyanids. (M)'(CN). Use KCN.

45. H_2SO_4 causes the evolution of HCN gas, which is recognized by its odor of bitter almonds or peach blossoms.

46. Moisten a piece of filter paper with a freshly prepared alcoholic soln. of guaiacum; dip the paper into a very dilute soln. $CuSO_4$, and hold it over a vessel from which vapor of HCN is given off; the paper turns bright blue.

47. $AgNO_3$ gives a white ppt. (AgCN) if the reagent is in excess. The ppt. is sol. in NH_4HO, insol. in HNO_3, and very sol. in excess of KCN.

48. Add NH_4HS to soln. and evaporate to dryness on water bath; add neutral Fe_2Cl_6 to residue: a deep red color.

49. KHO, and then soln. of $FeSO_4$, shake until it turns dark; add HCl just to acid reaction: a blue ppt. either immediately or after standing.

50. Add dil. soln. of picric acid, heat, and allow to cool: a deep red color.

* If the materials are not perfectly dry, colorless drops (of water) will condense.

	Ferrocyanids, $(M)^{iv}Fe(CN)_6$.	Ferricyanids, $(M)^{vi}[Fe(CN)_6]_2$.	Thiocyanates, $(M)'CNS$.
51.			
Fe_2Cl_6	dark blue ppt., insol. HCl, sol. $H_2C_2O_4$, with KHO turns brown.	green to brown color, no ppt.	blood-red color, destroyed by $HgCl_2$.
$FeSO_4$	light blue ppt., insol. HCl.	dark blue ppt.	
$CuSO_4$	chocolate ppt.	yellow ppt.	....
$AgNO_3$	white ppt., insol. in NH_4HO.	orange ppt., sol. in NH_4HO.	....

Nitrates. $(M)'NO_3$. Use dil. KNO_3.

52. $FeSO_4$. Add an equal bulk of H_2SO_4 to the soln. in a test-tube, agitate and cool, then with a simple pipette, *a*, Fig. 8, float soln. $FeSO_4$ on the mixture: a dark-brown layer forms between the two solutions, immediately if in strong, or after standing if in weak solutions.

53. Cu. Add some small pieces of Cu and H_2SO_4 to a soln. of nitrate, and heat: brown fumes are given off.

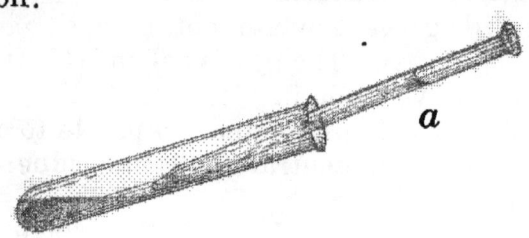

Fig. 8.

Nitric Acid. HNO_3.

54. The free acid responds to the $FeSO_4$ test for nitrates without the addition of H_2SO_4.

55. Moisten a crystal of brucin with the liquid: a bright carmin-red color. Nitrates respond to this test after addition of H_2SO_4.

56. Dissolve 252 pts. of mercuric cyanid and 266 pts. KI in H_2O, evaporate to crystallization; separate, and dry the crystals: a crystal introduced into nitric acid turns black.

57. Acidulate the (colorless) liquid with HCl (c. p.), and add 1-2 gtt. indigo-carmin soln.: the blue color is discharged.

Chlorates. (M)$'ClO_3$. Use $KClO_3$.

58. **Indigo soln.** To a cold soln. of chlorate add soln. indigo to a distinct blue, then add a few drops H_2SO_4: the blue color disappears.

Acetates. (M)$'(C_2H_3O_2)$. Use $Na(C_2H_3O_2)$.

59. H_2SO_4 causes the escape of acetic acid, which is recognized by its odor. If to the soln. of acetate a few drops of alcohol be added, then H_2SO_4, and heated: acetic ether will be given off, to be recognized also by its odor.

60. Fe_2Cl_6 gives a deep red coloration if neither solution contains free acid. Add HCl: the color changes to yellow.

Oxids. [Hydroxids.] (M)$'HO$—(M)$''H_2O_2$.

61. The oxids of As, Na, K, Ca and Ba are soluble in water, being converted into hydroxids. Oxids are determined by negative results, *i.e.*, by the exclusion of the acid residues.

Sulfids. (M)$''S$. Use $(NH_4)HS$.

62. H_2SO_4 with heat causes the evolution of the gas H_2S, with characteristic odor, and which will blacken paper moistened with $Pb(C_2H_3O_2)_2$.

63. AgNO₃ gives a black ppt. (Ag₂S), insol. in HNO₃. A drop of the original solution on a bright silver coin gives a dark spot.

64. Fe₂Cl₆ gives a black ppt. (FeS).

Sulfites. (M)″SO₃. Use Na₂SO₃.

65. H₂SO₄ with heat disengages the gas SO₂—recognized by its suffocating odor, and the change to a green color of a drop of K₂Cr₂O₇ held on a stirring-rod within the tube; or by its action on paper moistened with starch paste and iodic acid, which turns blue.

66. AgNO₃ gives a white ppt. (Ag₂SO₃) if the reagent be in excess. The ppt. is very sol. in excess of sulfite, and sol. also in HNO₃.

67. BaCl₂ gives a white ppt. (BaSO₃), sol. in HCl (c. p.). If chlorin water be now added, a white ppt., insol. in acids, is produced.

68. CaCl₂ gives a white ppt. (CaSO₃) in concentrated solutions (5 per cent.), sol. in HCl.

69. Fe₂Cl₆ gives a red-brown color if neutral.

70. Zn and HCl cause the production of H₂S gas, which gives a brown or black stain on paper moistened with Pb(C₂H₃O₂)₂ held at the mouth of the tube.

Sulfates. (M)″SO₄. Use dil. H₂SO₄+2KHO.

71. BaCl₂ or **Ba(NO₃)₂** gives a white ppt. (BaSO₄) which is insol. in acids.

72. CaCl₂, either immediately or on dilution with two volumes of alcohol, gives a white ppt. (CaSO₄), insol. in dil. HCl or dil. HNO₃.

Sulfuric Acid. H₂SO₄.

73. The free acid answers to the above tests for sulfates.

74. Add very small fragment lead chromate, boil, filter; add KI (1 gtt.) and carbon bisulfid (2 to 3 gtt.), and agitate: the CS_2 is colored violet. Agitate another portion of the liquid with CS_2 after addition of KI: no violet color should be produced.

75. Dissolve 3 per cent. of cane-sugar in the liquid, moisten a piece of filter paper with it, and dry: the paper turns brown or black.

76. Moisten a little veratrin with the liquid, and evaporate over the water-bath to dryness: a crimson color.

Thiosulfates. (M)″S_2O_3. Use $Na_2S_2O_3$.

77. H_2SO_4 in cold solutions (not too dilute) deposits S, and becomes green on addition of $K_2Cr_2O_7$.

78. $AgNO_3$ gives a white ppt. ($Ag_2S_2O_3$), which becomes black on standing or heating. The ppt. is sol. in excess of thiosulfate.

79. Fe_2Cl_6 gives a reddish-violet color.

Carbonates. (M)″CO_3. Use $(NH_4)_2CO_3$.

80. H_2SO_4 causes evolution of gas CO_2 with effervescence. A drop of CaH_2O_2 on the end of a stirring-rod held in the gas in the test-tube, turns milky. Or hold tube upright until effervescence ceases, then pour the *heavy gas* into a test-tube containing about one cent. of CaH_2O_2, agitate: a white ppt. forms.

81. $AgNO_3$ gives a white ppt. (Ag_2CO_3), sol. in dil. HNO_3.

82. $BaCl_2$ gives a white ppt. ($BaCO_3$), sol. in HCl (c. p.), insol. in NH_4Cl.

83. $CaCl_2$ gives a white ppt. ($CaCO_3$), sol. in acids, insol. in NH_4Cl.

OXALATES—TARTRATES. 17

84. Fe_2Cl_6 gives a reddish ppt. ($Fe_2[CO_3]_3$), sol. in HCl, insol. in NH_4HO or KHO.

Oxalates. (M)''C_2O_4. Use $H_2C_2O_4$ or $(NH_4)_2C_2O_4$.

85. H_2SO_4 on a solid oxalate disengages the gases CO and CO_2; the first detected by burning with a blue flame when ignited, and the CO_2 by its action with CaH_2O_2. The solid does not blacken.

86. $AgNO_3$ gives a white ppt. ($Ag_2C_2O_4$), sol. in dil. HNO_3 and in NH_4HO.

87. $BaCl_2$ in neutral solutions of oxalates (neutralize $H_2C_2O_4$ with NH_4HO) gives a white ppt. (BaC_2O_4), sol. in HCl (c. p.) or HNO_3, insol. in NH_4Cl.

88. $CaCl_2$ gives a white ppt. (CaC_2O_4), sol. in HCl or HNO_3, insol. in $H(C_2H_3O_2)$ or NH_4HO.

Tartrates. (M)''$C_4H_4O_6$. Use $KNa(C_4H_4O_6)$.

89. H_2SO_4 on solid tartrate blackens immediately on warming.

90. $AgNO_3$ gives a white ppt. ($Ag_2C_4H_4O_6$) in neutral solution, add dil. NH_4HO until nearly dissolved, place in sunlight or in a vessel of water, which heat slowly up to about 60°: a silver mirror forms in the tube. The white ppt. is sol. in dil. HNO_3.

91. $BaCl_2$ gives a white ppt. ($BaC_4H_4O_6$), sol. in HCl (c. p.), HNO_3, $H(C_2H_3O_2)$, or in NH_4Cl.

92. $CaCl_2$ gives a white ppt. ($CaC_4H_4O_6$), which collect, wash, dissolve in soln. KHO, and apply heat: a white ppt.

93. CaH_2O_2 gives a white ppt., sol. in excess of $H_2(C_4H_4O_6)$.

94. To a neutral or alkaline soln. add a few drops $K_2Mn_2O_8$, and heat slowly: the color is discharged and MnO precipitated.

Phosphates. $(M)'''PO_4$. Use HNa_2PO_4.

95. $AgNO_3$ gives a yellow ppt. (HAg_2PO_4), sol. in HNO_3 (c. p.) and in NH_4HO.

96. $BaCl_2$ gives a white ppt. ($Ba_3[PO_4]_2$), sol. in acids, insol. in NH_4Cl.

97. $CaCl_2$ gives a white ppt. ($Ca_3[PO_4]_2$), sol. in HCl or $H(C_2H_3O_2)$, insol. in NH_4HO or NH_4Cl.

98. Fe_2Cl_6 gives a yellowish-white ppt. ($Fe_2[PO_4]_2$), sol. in HCl, insol. in $H(C_2H_3O_2)$, NH_4HO, or KHO.

99. $MgSO_4$ with NH_4Cl and NH_4HO gives a white ppt. ($Mg[NH_4]PO_4$), sol. in acids, almost insol. in NH_4HO.

100. $H(NH_4)MoO_4$ in HNO_3 gives a yellow ppt., which may be hastened by warming; sol. in alkalies, insol. in HNO_3.

Arsenates. $(M)'''AsO_4$. Use HNa_2AsO_4.

101. $AgNO_3$ gives a brick-red ppt. (Ag_3AsO_4), sol. in HNO_3 or NH_4HO, insol. in KHO.

102. $BaCl_2$ gives a faint white ppt. ($Ba_3[AsO_4]_2$), sol. in HCl or HNO_3, insol. in $H(C_2H_3O_2)$.

103. $CaCl_2$ gives a white ppt. ($Ca_3[AsO_4]_2$), sol. in HCl or HNO_3, insol. in NH_4HO.

104. Fe_2Cl_6 gives a yellowish-white ppt. ($Fe_2[AsO_4]_2$), sol. in HCl, HNO_3, or NH_4HO, insol. in KHO.

105. $MgSO_4$ same as with phosphates (see § 99).

106. $H(NH_4)MoO_4$ gives a yellow ppt.; same as for phosphates, except that it appears only on boiling.

107. $CuSO_4$, in neutral soln., gives a bluish-green ppt. ($Cu_3[AsO_4]_2$), sol. in HCl, HNO_3, or NH_4HO, insol. in KHO.

108. H_2S. Add HCl and boil, then pass H_2S through the hot soln.: a yellow ppt. (As_2S_3) forms slowly.

109. (For **Arsenites**, (M)'''AsO_3, this last test may be applied to the filtrate obtained after separating the ppt. with $MgSO_4$: it gives a yellow ppt. (As_2S_3) immediately. **$AgNO_3$** in solns. made slightly alkaline with NH_4HO: a yellow ppt. [Ag_3AsO_3], sol. in NH_4HO, insol. in HCl. With $CuSO_4$ in similar solns. a yellowish-green ppt. [$HCuAsO_3$].)
Reinsch and **Marsh** tests. See §§ 398, 399.

Antimonates. (M)'''SbO_4.

110. $AgNO_3$. Add KHO to distinct alkaline reaction, then $AgNO_3$, which gives a brown ppt., sol. in NH_4HO. (Antimonites give a dark ppt., insol. in NH_4HO.)

111. KI. Acidify with HCl, warm, and add soln. KI: a brown color results, which on addition of starch soln. turns blue. (Antimonites fail to give this reaction.)

112. H_2S. Acidify with HCl and add soln. H_2S: an orange-red ppt. (SbS_3), sol. in warm KHO or in NH_4HS.

113. Reinsch and **Marsh** tests. See §§ 398, 399, 406, and 407.

Borates. (M)''BO_3. Use $Na_2B_4O_7$.

114. $AgNO_3$ gives a white ppt., sol. in HNO_3 or NH_4HO.

115. $BaCl_2$ in concentrated solns. gives a white ppt., sol. in HCl (c. p.) and in alkaline salts.

CITRATES. 20

116. $CaCl_2$ in concentrated solns. gives a white ppt., sol. in HCl or NH_4Cl, insol. in NH_4HO.
117. Fe_2Cl_6 gives a yellow ppt., sol. in excess of reagent or in HCl, insol. in NH_4HO.
118. Turmeric paper moistened with a borate and dried turns brown.
119. Flame test. Concentrate on a watch-glass, add a drop of HCl, and examine with a clean platinum or iron wire: gives a green coloration.

Citrates. (M)'''$C_6H_5O_7$. Use $H_3C_6H_5O_7$.

120. H_2SO_4 on solid citrate and heated, blackens after a time.
121. $AgNO_3$ gives a white ppt., sol. in HNO_3 (c. p.) or in NH_4HO. This ppt. will blacken on prolonged boiling.
122. $BaCl_2$ in concentrated solns. gives a white ppt., sol. in HCl (c. p.), insol. in NH_4Cl.
123. $CaCl_2$ in neutral soln. gives a white ppt. on heating, sol. in HCl or $H(C_2H_3O_2)$, insol. in KHO.
124. $C_4H_2O_2$ gives a white ppt. on heating, which redissolves on cooling.

125. SUMMARY OF REACTIONS OF ACID RESIDUES

(in neutral solutions, see § 32).

Primary tests. Secondary tests.	Refer to §§	H_2SO_4. Heat.	$AgNO_3$. Dil. HNO_3, NH_4HO.	$BaCl_2$ or $CaCl_2$. HCl, $H(C_2H_3O_2)$, NH_4HO, NH_4Cl.	Fe_2Cl_6.
Chlorids	33		white ppt.		
Bromids	37		" "		
Iodids	39		yellow "		
Cyanids	45	HCN gas, odor.	white "		
Nitrates	52	(Add equal bulk H_2SO_4, cool, float strong cold $FeSO_4$; dark-brown layer.) § 44			
Chlorates	58	(Add cold soln. indigo to distinct blue, add H_2SO_4; blue color discharged.)			
Acetates	59	$H(C_2H_3O_2)$ vapor.	white ppt.		red color.
Oxids	61	(Determined by negative results).			
Sulfids	62	H_2S gas.	black ppt.	white ppt.	black ppt.
Sulfites	65	SO_2 gas.	white "	" insol. acids	red-brown color.
Sulfates	71			" insol. NH_4Cl	
Carbonates	80	CO_2 gas	white ppt.	" "	red-brown ppt.
Oxalates	85	CO and CO_2 gas.	" "	" sol. "	
Tartrates	89	solid blackens.	" "	" insol. "	
Phosphates	95		yellow "	" "	yellow ppt.
Arsenates	101		brown-red ppt.	" "	" "
Antimonates	111		brown ppt.		
Borates	115		white "	" sol. NH_4Cl	yellow ppt.
Citrates	121	solid blackens.			

ACIDIC ELEMENTS GROUPED FOR ANALYTICAL PURPOSES.

126. Acid Residues grouped according to reactions. Add strong H_2SO_4; if no gas evolved, apply heat.

Cyanids, gas, odor.	Add $AgNO_3$ to original; if ppt., filter; test ppt. with dil. HNO_3; test filtrate as below.	
Acetates, " "		
Sulfids, " "	Chlorids white ⎫	Add $BaCl_2$ to original or to filtrate from $AgNO_3$ ppt.; then HCl (c. p.).
Sulfites, " "	Bromids " ⎬ ppt. insol.	
Carbonates, effervescence.......	Iodids yellow ⎭	
Oxalates, effervescence, if con.....	Phosphates yellow ⎫	Sulfate, white ppt. insol.
*Tartrates, blacken.	Arsenates red ⎬ ppt. sol.	If not, test for nitrates, chlorates.
*Citrates, "	Borates white ⎭	
	Antimonates brown	If not, is an oxid or hydroxid.
*Solids.		

REACTIONS OF THE MORE COMMON BASES.

127. The elements, which form bases, are grouped, for purposes of analysis, according to their characteristic precipitations with H_2S, in acid solutions; NH_4HS, in neutral solutions; $(NH_4)_2CO_3$, in alkaline solutions; and flame colorations, as follows:

GROUP I.
K. Na. NH_4. [Li. Cs. Rb.]

GROUP II.
Ba. Sr. Ca. Mg.

GROUP III.
Al. Cr. [Be. Th. Zr. Yt. Ce. La. D. Ti. Ta. Cb.]

GROUP IV.
Zn. Mn. Ni. Co. Fe. [U. Tl. In. Ga. V.]

GROUP V.
Ag. Hg. Pb. Cu. Bi. Cd. [Pd. Rh. Os. Ru.]

GROUP VI.
Au. Pt. Sn. Sb. As. [Gr. Ir. Mo. W. Te. Se.]

REACTIONS OF THE MORE COMMON BASES. 23

H_2S Test. Use $Pb(C_2H_3O_2)_2$.

128. Take 2 cent. water in a test-tube, add about 10 drops of soln. of substance, add few drops HCl. (If HCl gives a ppt., then repeat, using HNO_3 instead of HCl.) Add to the acidified soln. one-half its bulk of H_2S soln., agitate and warm. Or, in place of H_2S soln., the gas H_2S may be bubbled through the mixture until pptn. is complete. Collect the ppt. on a filter and wash with hot water. Transfer small portions of ppt. with stirring-rod to watch-glasses, and apply secondary tests, as NH_4HS or HNO_3. Is insol. in former and sol. in latter. § 148.

The H_2S solution decomposes on standing, and must be fresh and strong to give its reactions.

NH_4HS Test. Use $FeSO_4$.

129. Take 2 cent. water, add about 10 drops of substance, add 10–15 drops NH_4Cl and 2–3 drops NH_4HO, or more if necessary to neutralize or render slightly alkaline; then add NH_4HS as long as a ppt. forms. Collect, wash, and test as in the H_2S test.

$(NH_4)_2CO_3$ Test. Use $CaCl_2$.

130. Take 2 cent. water and about 10 drops of substance, add 10–15 drops NH_4Cl and 4–5 drops NH_4HO, or to distinct alkaline reaction; add $(NH_4)_2CO_3$, and test solubility of ppts. directly in test-tubes.

Flame Test. Use KHO.

131 Concentrate about 10 drops of substance in a watch-glass, held in fingers and passed back and forth through a very small flame. Add when cool

MANGANESE—IRON. 24

one drop HCl, moisten a piece of clean platinum or iron wire in the substance and bring to the side of the flame near the mouth of the burner. Examine with blue glass or indigo prism. Flame colored violet.

Manganese. Mn″ iv 54. Use $MnCl_2$ (fresh soln. Oxidize with HNO_3 for manganic.)

132. NH_4HS gives a pink or tawny ppt. (MnS), sol. in acids, insol. in NH_4Cl. (Perform test as in § 129.)

133. $(NH_4)_2CO_3$ gives a white ppt. ($MnCO_3$), sol. in HCl or NH_4Cl, insol. in NH_4HO or KHO.

134. **KHO** gives a white ppt. (MnH_2O_2) changing to brown, insol. in excess of reagent or NH_4HO.

Manganous.	Manganic.
135. **KCN** gives a rose ppt $(Mn[CN]_2)$, with brown solution if in excess.	light-brown ppt. $(Mn_2-[CN]_6)$.
136. $K_4Fe(CN)_6$, faint reddish-white ppt. $(Mn_2-Fe[CN]_6)$, sol. in HCl.	greenish ppt. $([Mn_2]_2-3Fe[CN]_4)$.
137. $K_4Fe_2(CN)_{12}$, brown ppt. $(Mn_3Fe_2[CN]_{12})$, insol. in HCl.	brown ppt. $([Mn_2]Fe_2-[CN]_{12})$.

Iron. Fe‴·iv 55.9. Use $FeSO_4$ and Fe_2Cl_6.

138. NH_4HS gives a black ppt. (FeS), insol. in excess, sol. in HCl, insol. in NH_4Cl or $H(C_2H_3O_2)$.

Ferrous.	Ferric.
139. $(NH_4)_2CO_3$ or **KHO** greenish white ppt., insol. in excess, changes to green, then to rust, sol. in HCl, insol. in NH_4HO.	rust-colored ppt. $(Fe_2-[CO_3]_3$ or $Fe_2H_6O_6)$, with same solubilities.

ALUMINIUM—LEAD.

Ferrous.

140. NH_4HO in absence of NH_4 salts, greenish ppt. (FeH_2O_2), sol. in NH_4Cl.

141. $K_4Fe(CN)_6$ white ppt., changing to blue in air, insol. in HCl.

142. $K_6Fe_2(CN)_{12}$ blue ppt., sol. in KHO, insol. in HCl.

Ferric.

rust ppt. ($Fe_2H_6O_6$), sol. in NH_4Cl.

blue (Prussian blue) ppt., sol. in NH_4HO or KHO, insol. in HCl.

green soln., add $SnCl_2$: a blue ppt.

143. KCNS gives a dark-red color, prevented by $C_4H_6O_6$ or $C_6H_8O_7$.

144. Tannin gives a blue-black color.

Aluminium. $Al^{iv}(''')$ **27.02.** Use $(NH_4)_2SO_4Al_2(SO_4)_3$.

145. NH_4HS gives a white ppt. (Al_2S_3), sol. in HCl or KHO, insol. in NH_4Cl.

146. $(NH_4)_2CO_3$ or NH_4HO gives a white ppt. ($Al_2H_6O_6$), insol. in excess, sol. in HCl or KHO, insol. in NH_4Cl.

147. KHO gives a white ppt. ($Al_2H_6O_6$), sol. in excess. To a part add HCl gradually until neutral: ppt. reappears. Add more acid: ppt. disappears.

Lead. Pb''^{-iv} **206.92.** Use $Pb(C_2H_3O_2)_2$.

148. H_2S gives a black ppt. (PbS), insol. in NH_4HS or cold dil. acids, sol. in hot HNO_3.

149. NH_4HS gives a black ppt. (PbS), insol. in excess or HCl, sol. in hot HNO_3.

150. $(NH_4)_2CO_3$ or NH_4HO gives a white ppt. ($PbCO_3$ or PbH_2O_2), insol. in excess, sol. in HNO_3, insol. in H_2SO_4.

151. KHO gives a white ppt. (PbH$_2$O$_2$), sol. in excess or HNO$_3$, insol. in HCl or H$_2$SO$_4$.

152. HCl gives a white ppt. (PbCl$_2$), if not too dilute, sol. in boiling water.

152a. H$_2$SO$_4$ gives a white ppt. (PbSO$_4$), sol. in (NH$_4$)$_2$C$_4$H$_4$O$_6$.

153. KI gives a yellow ppt. (PbI$_2$), sol. in a large excess of boiling water. Decant mixture after pptn. into small flask, add H$_2$O to about one-half full, make a paper holder of folded writing-paper, bend around the neck of flask; boil for a minute or two, then filter into beaker and set aside to cool: flaky yellow crystals of PbI$_2$ should appear.

154. K$_2$CrO$_4$ gives a yellow ppt. (PbCrO$_4$), sol. in KHO.

Bismuth. Bi''' 206.5. Use Bi(NO$_3$)$_3$ + HNO$_3$.

155. H$_2$S and **NH$_4$HS** give reactions very similar to those of lead (Bi$_2$S$_3$).

156. (NH$_4$)$_2$CO$_3$, NH$_4$HO, or **KHO** gives a white ppt. (Bi$_2$[CO$_3$]$_3$ or BiH$_3$O$_3$), insol. in excess, and which turns yellow on boiling. The ppt. is sol. in HCl, HNO$_3$, or H$_2$SO$_4$.

157. K$_4$Fe(CN)$_6$ gives a yellowish ppt. (Bi$_4$[Fe(CN)$_6$]$_3$), sol. in HCl, insol. in H$_2$SO$_4$.

158. K$_6$Fe$_2$(CN)$_{12}$, a yellowish ppt. (Bi$_2$Fe$_2$[CN]$_{12}$), sol. in HCl, HNO$_3$; insol. in NH$_4$HO, KHO, HC$_2$H$_3$O$_2$, H$_2$SO$_4$.

159. KI gives a brown ppt. (BiI$_3$), sol. in excess.

160. Infusion Galls gives an orange ppt.

161. Reinsch test gives reduction without sublimation. See § 398.

162. H$_2$O gives a white ppt. Add NH$_4$HO to strong solution, collect the white ppt. on a filter, wash, dissolve with hot HNO_3, dil. with equal vol. H_2O, and allow the drops from the funnel to fall into clear water : a white ppt.

Tin. Sn''-iv 117.7. Use $SnCl_2$(+ HNO_3 for stannic).

Stannous.	Stannic.
163. H_2S a brown ppt. (SnS), sol. in NH_4HS, KHO, and hot HCl, insol. in HNO_3, but turns white on boiling ($H_2Sn_5O_{11}$).	yellow ppt. (SnS_2), with same solubilities.
164. NH_4HS a brown ppt. (SnS), sol. in excess.	yellow ppt. (SnS_2), sol. in excess.
165. $(NH_4)_2CO_3$ a white ppt. ($Sn[OH]_2$), insol. in excess, sol. in strong acids or KHO.	white ppt. ($Sn[CO_3]_2$), with same solubilities.
166. NH_4HO a white ppt. ($Sn[OH_2]$), insol. in excess.	white ppt. ($Sn[OH]_4$), sparingly sol. in excess.
167. KHO a white ppt. ($Sn[OH]_2$), sol. in excess; on boiling deposits tin.	white ppt. ($Sn[OH]_4$), sol. in excess.
168. $K_4Fe(CN)_6$ a white gelatinous ppt. ($Sn_2Fe[CN]_6$).	same.
169. $HgCl_2$ in excess a white ppt. (Hg_2Cl_2).	
170. Zn in soln. acidified with HCl causes a deposit of Sn.	**171.** $Na_2S_2O_3$ gives a yellow ppt. ($Sn[S_2O_3]_2$) on heating.

Lithium. Li' 7. Use LiCl.

172. $(NH_4)_2CO_3$ gives in concentrated soln. and in absence of NH_4 salts a white ppt. (Li_2CO_3).

SODIUM—POTASSIUM.

173. HNa_2PO_4 gives a white ppt. (HLi_2PO_4) in neutral or alkaline solutions, sol. in acids and in NH_4Cl.

174. Flame test gives red, best seen through the thin part of an indigo prism.

Sodium. Na′ 22.998. Use NaCl.

175. H_2SiF_6 gives a gelatinous ppt. (Na_2SiF_6), if soln. not too dilute, sol in strong acids.

176. $H_2K_2Sb_2O_7$ gives a white, flocculent ppt. ($H_2Na_2Sb_2O_7$) in neutral solns. and in absence of metals other than K and Li; the ppt. becomes crystalline on standing.

The solution of $H_2K_2Sb_2O_7$ must be freshly prepared. Dissolve a little of the solid in 1-2 cent. of boiling water, filter, and use filtrate.

177. HIO_4 in excess gives a white ppt. ($NaIO_4$) in not too dilute solns.

178. Flame is enlarged and colored yellow.

Potassium. K′ 39.137. Use KCl.

179. $PtCl_4$ with a drop or two of HCl gives a yellow ppt. (K_2PtCl_6), sparingly sol. in H_2O.

180. $C_4H_6O_6$ gives a white ppt. ($HKC_4H_4O_6$) in concentrated solns., sol. in strong acids and alkalies.

181. H_2SiF_6 gives a translucent, gelatinous ppt. (K_2SiF_6), which forms slowly and is sol. in strong alkalies.

182. HIO_4 gives a white ppt. (KIO_4), sparingly sol. in H_2O, insol. in alcohol.

183. Phosphomolybdic acid gives a white ppt., which forms slowly.

184. Flame is colored violet, seen through blue glass or indigo prism.

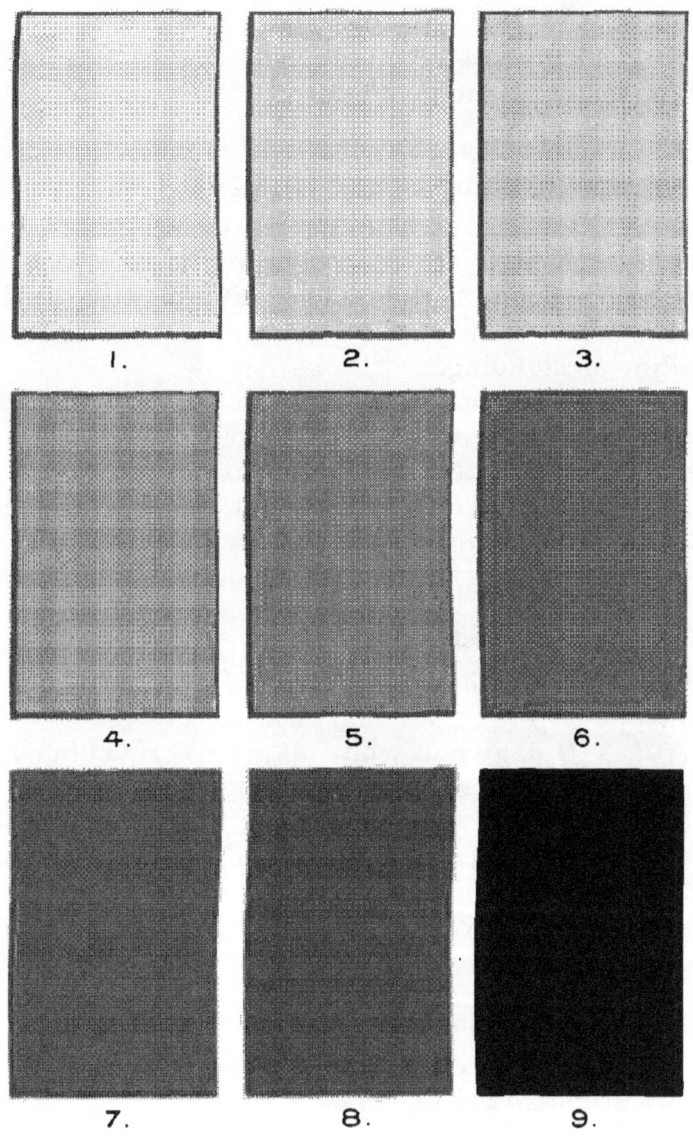

COLORS OF URINE.

Ammonium. (NH₄)′ 18.044. Use NH₄Cl.

185. Salts of ammonium are volatile at high temperatures.

186. $PtCl_4$ gives a yellow, crystalline ppt. ($[NH_4]_2PtCl_6$) in concentrated solns.

187. $HNaC_4H_4O_6$ gives a white, crystalline ppt. ($H[NH_4]C_4H_4O_6$) if not too dilute.

·188. KHO and heat cause the evolution of ammonia gas, which is recognized by its odor, action on litmus, union with vapor of HCl in form of a white cloud.

Silver. Ag′ 107.675. Use AgNO₃.

189. H_2S or NH_4HS gives a black ppt. (Ag_2S), insol. in NH_4HS or HCl, sol. in hot HNO_3.

190. $(NH_4)_2CO_3$ gives a white ppt. (Ag_2CO_3), sol. in excess, in HNO_3, H_2SO_4, or NH_4HO.

191. KHO gives a brown ppt. (AgHO), insol. in excess or HCl, sol. in HNO_3, H_2SO_4, or NH_4HO.

192. NH_4HO gives a brown ppt. (AgHO) in neutral solns., sol. in slight excess,.insol. in HCl or KHO.

193. HCl gives a white, curdy ppt. (AgCl), sol. in NH_4HO, insol. in HNO_3.

194. KBr gives a yellowish-white ppt (AgBr), changing to black, insol. in acids, sol. in NH_4HO.

195. KI same as with KBr, except less soluble in NH_4HO (AgI).

Calcium. Ca″ 40. Use CaCl₂.

196. NH_4HS gives a white ppt. if the Ca salt is a phosphate, oxalate, or fluorid.

197. $(NH_4)_2CO_3$ in neutral soln. gives a white ppt. ($CaCO_3$), insol. in excess or H_2SO_4, sol. in HCl.

198. $(NH_4)_2C_2O_4$ gives a white ppt. (CaC_2O_4), insol. in $C_2H_4O_2$ or NH_4HO, sol. in HCl.

199. H_2SO_4 gives a white ppt. ($CaSO_4$), either immediately or on dilution with three volumes of alcohol; very sparingly sol. in H_2O, sol. in $Na_2S_2O_3$, soon turning yellowish-white (S).

200. Na_2WO_4 gives a dense white ppt. ($CaWO_4$), even in dil. soln.

201. Flame is colored a reddish yellow.

Barium. Ba" 136.8. Use $BaCl_2$.

202. $(NH_4)_2CO_3$ in neutral solns. gives a white ppt. ($BaCO_3$), insol. in excess or H_2SO_4, sol. in HCl or $C_2H_4O_2$.

203. HNa_2PO_4 gives a white ppt. ($Ca_3[PO_4]_2$), insol. in excess, NH_4HO, or KHO, sol. in HCl or $C_2H_4O_2$.

204. H_2SO_4 gives a white ppt. ($BaSO_4$), insol. in strong acids.

205. Flame is colored a greenish yellow.

Magnesium. Mg" 24. Use $MgSO_4$.

206. $(NH_4)_2CO_3$ gives a slight ppt. ($3[MgCO_3]$-MgH_2O_2) from hot conc. solns. in absence of NH_4 salts.

207. Na_2CO_3 or K_2CO_3 gives a white ppt. ($3[MgCO_3]$-MgH_2O_2), best from hot solns.; prevented by presence of NH_4 salts.

208. NH_4HO gives a voluminous white ppt. (MgH_2O_2) from neutral solns., insol. in excess, very sol. in NH_4Cl.

209. KHO or NaHO gives a white ppt. (MgH_2O_2) from warm solns.; prevented by NH_4 salts and certain organic substances.

210. HNa_2PO_4 gives a white ppt. ($Mg_3[PO_4]_2$) from hot and not too dilute solns.

211. H_2CrO_4 with NH_4HO gives a white ppt. [$MgCrO_4$], not formed in presence of NH_4 salts.

212. There is no pptn. with $(NH_4)_2CO_3$ in presence of NH_4Cl, which is added to the $(NH_4)_2CO_3$ tests for Ca and Ba, §§ 197, 202, to prevent a ppt. (MgH_2O_2) when Ca and Ba are tested for in presence of Mg.

Zinc. Zn″ 64.9. Use ZnSO$_4$.

213. H_2S in neutral solns. gives a white ppt. (ZnS). In presence of an excess of a mineral acid this ppt. is prevented, unless $Na(C_2H_3O_2)$ be also present.

214. NH_4HS gives a white ppt. (ZnS), insol. in excess, KHO, NH_4HO, or $C_2H_4O_2$, sol. in dil. mineral acids.

215. $(NH_4)_2CO_3$ gives a white, gelatinous ppt. $(ZnCO_3)$, sol. in excess, HCl, NH_4HO, KHO, or NH_4Cl.

216. K_2CO_3 or Na_2CO_3 gives a white ppt. $(ZnCO_3)$ in absence of an NH_4 salt.

217. NH_4HO, KHO, or $NaHO$ gives a white ppt. (ZnH_2O_2), sol. in excess.

218. HNa_2PO_4 gives, in absence of NH_4 salts, a white ppt. $(Zn_3[PO_4]_2)$, sol. in acids or alkalies.

219. $K_4Fe(CN)_6$ gives a white ppt. $(Zn_2Fe[CN]_6)$, sol. in NH_4HO or KHO, insol. in HCl.

Copper. Cu″ 63.2. Use CuSO$_4$.

220. H_2S or NH_4HS gives a black ppt. (CuS), sparingly sol. in NH_4HS, sol. in hot concentrated HNO_3 and in KCN.

221. $(NH_4)_2CO_3$ or NH_4HO gives a pale blue ppt. (CuH_2O_2), sol. with deep blue color in excess.

222. KHO, NaHO, K_2CO_3, or Na_2CO_3 gives a pale blue ppt. $(CuH_2O_2$ or $CuCO_3 + CuH_2O_2)$, insol. in excess. On boiling with KHO the ppt. turns black $(3CuO, H_2O)$.

MERCURY. 32

223. **KCN** gives a greenish-yellow ppt. (Cu[CN]$_2$), sol in slight excess, HCl, HNO$_3$, or NH$_4$HO, insol. in KHO.

224. **K$_4$Fe(CN)$_6$** gives a chestnut-brown ppt. (Cu$_2$Fe[CN]$_6$), insol. in excess or weak acids, decolorized by KHO.

225. **Fe.** A clean knife-blade or needle held in an acidulated soln. of Cu becomes coated with metallic Cu.

226. **Flame** is colored green.

Mercury. Hg″ 199.7. Use Hg$_2$(NO$_3$)$_2$ and HgCl$_2$.

Mercurous.	Mercuric.
227. HCl a white ppt. (Hg$_2$Cl$_2$), insol. in H$_2$O or in acids, turns black with NH$_4$HO.	
228. H$_2$S a black ppt. (HgS + Hg), insol. in NH$_4$HS, HCl, or HNO$_3$, partly sol. in boiling HNO$_3$, sol. in aqua regia.	ppt. at first white, then orange, then black (HgS + HgCl$_2$).
229. NH$_4$HS a black ppt. (HgS + Hg), insol. in excess.	ppt. white to black, insol. in excess, except in presence of organic matter.
230. (NH$_4$)$_2$CO$_3$ a dark gray ppt., sol. in hot HNO$_3$, insol. in H$_2$SO$_4$.	white ppt., sol. in great excess of reagent, in H$_2$SO$_4$, or in NH$_4$HO (K$_2$CO$_3$ gives a red ppt.).
231. KHO a dark gray ppt. (Hg$_2$O), insol. in excess, HCl, or NH$_4$HO, sol. in hot HNO$_3$.	yellowish-red ppt. (HgO), sol. in HCl, HNO$_3$, or NH$_4$HO.

MERCURY. 33

Mercurous.

232. NH_4HO same as KHO.

233. $K_4Fe(CN)_6$ a white, gelatinous ppt.

234. KI a greenish ppt. (Hg_2I_2), converted by excess into Hg, which is deposited, and HgI, which dissolves.

235. Reinsch test, see §§ 398 and 412.

Mercuric.

white ppt. (NH_2HgCl), slightly sol. in excess, strong acids, or NH_4Cl.

white ppt. changing to blue.

yellow to salmon to red ppt. (HgI_2), easily sol. in excess of KI or in great excess of the mercuric salt.

236. SUMMARY OF THE REACTIONS OF THE BASES.

Preparatory. Primary tests. Secondary.	Refer to §	HCl or HNO₃, H₂S § 128, NH₄HS or KHO.	NH₄Cl+NH₄HO NH₄HS § 129, add excess.	NH₄Cl+NH₄HO (NH₄)₂CO₃ § 130, add excess.	KHO add excess.	NH₄HO add excess.	K₄Fe(CN)₆ add HCl.
Manganese	132	....	flesh color, insol.	white, insol.	white to brown, insol.	white to brown, insol.	red-white, sol.
Iron (ous)	138	....	black, insol.	white green to rust, insol.	same as (NH₄)₂CO₃	same as (NH₄)₂CO₃	white to blue, insol.
" (ic)		....	" "	rust, insol.	same as (NH₄)₂CO₃	same as (NH₄)₂CO₃	deep blue, insol.
Aluminium	145	....	white, "	white, insol.	white, sol.	white, insol	white.
Lead	148	black, insol.	black, "	" "	" insol.	" "	" insol.
Bismuth	155	....	" "	" "	" "	" "	yellowish, insol.
Tin (ous)	163	brown, sol.	brown, sol	" "	" sol.	white to olive, insol.	white, insol.
" (ic)		yellow, "	yellow, "	" "	....	white, sp. sol.	"
Lithium	172	(Concentrate, add HCl, heat on Pt wire in flame: a crimson-red color.)
Sodium	175	(" " " " " " " " an enlarged yellow flame.)
Potassium	179	(" " " " " " " " a violet color.)
(Ammonium)	185	(Heated with KHO gives off NH₃; odor and action on litmus.)
Silver	189	black, insol.	black, insol.	white, sol.	brown, insol.	pale brown, sol.	white, insol.
Calcium	196	....	....	" insol.	....	....	....
Barium	202	....	....	"	....	....	....
Magnesium	206	....	white, insol.	white, sol.	white, insol.	white, insol.	....
Zinc	213	....	" "	" "	" sol	" sol	white, sp. sol.
Copper	220	black, insol.	black, sl. sol.	green-blue, sol. to blue soln.	pale blue to brown on boilg.	pale blue soln.	mahogany, insol.
Mercury (ous)	227	" "	" insol.	dark gray, insol	dark gray, insol	black, insol.	white, insol.
" (ic)		white to black, insol.	white to black, insol.	white, sp. sol.	yellow, insol	white, sp. sol.	white to blue, sol.

237. Bases grouped according to behavior with grouping reagents.

Precipitated by HCl: (Consult §§ 128-131).

Pb	If not, add H_2S in excess, precipitated:		
Ag, Hg(ous) § 238	Bi, Sn(ous), Cu, Hg(ic) } brown or black, § 239. As, Sn(ic) } yellow, § 240. Sb, orange.		
	A yellowish-white ppt. with H_2S is sulfur.		
	If not, apply NH_4HS test to original solution, precipitated:		
	Mn, pink. Fe, black. Al } white, Zn } § 241.		
		If not, try $(NH_4)_2CO_3$ test with original solution.	
		Ca } white, Ba } § 242.	If not, try the flame test with original substance. Li, crimson. Na, yellow. K, violet.
		If not, add HNa_2PO_4. Mg, white.	
			If not, test for $\dot{N}H_4$, § 188.

238. Collect ppt. by HCl on a filter, wash, transfer a portion to a watch-glass, add a drop or two NH_4HO:

    the ppt. does not change.................**Pb.**
    the ppt. dissolves.........................**Ag.**
    the ppt. turns black...............**Hg** (ous).

239. Collect the black ppt. by H_2S, wash with hot water, transfer to watch-glasses, and test with NH_4HS and heat:

    the ppt. dissolves..................**Sn** (ous).

Test another portion with hot HNO_3:

    The ppt. does not dissolve..........**Hg** (ic).

Test the original solution with NH_4HO:

    a blue ppt., sol. in excess, dark-blue soln.....................................**Cu.**
    with NH_4HO a white ppt. (verify by § 162) ....**Bi.**

240. Collect the yellow ppt., wash, transfer to watch-glass or test-tube, and warm with $(NH_4)_2CO_3$:

    the ppt. dissolves........................**As.**
    the ppt. does not dissolve..........**Sn** (ic).

241. Collect and test the white ppt. by NH_4HS with NH_4HO:

    the ppt. is soluble. The original soln. gives white ppt. with NH_4HO, sol. in excess, **Zn.**
    the ppt. is insoluble. The original soln. gives white ppt. with NH_4HO, insol. in excess.......................................**Al.**

242. Collect the white ppt. by $(NH_4)_2CO_3$, dissolve with $C_2H_4O_2$, and add K_2CrO_4:

    a ppt. forms...............................**Ba.**
    a ppt. does not form....................**Ca.**

EXAMINATION OF MIXTURES OF SALTS SOLUBLE IN WATER.*

Determination of the Bases.†

243. Dissolve in water, note the reaction of the solution, and add HCl (if alkaline, to distinct acid reaction):

    a. No ppt. = absence of Ag, Hg (ous), or notable quantity of Pb. Pass on to § **244.**

    b. A white ppt. (the original soln: was neutral or acid): add HCl, drop by drop, until precipitation is complete, then 8–10 gtt. more, agitate, filter and wash ppt. twice, examine filtrate and washings according to § 244. Treat ppt. on filter with boiling H_2O; add H_2S to filtrate: a black ppt. .. **Lead.**

Treat ppt. on filter (if any remain) with NH_4HO:

    aa. It turns black........ **Mercury (ous).**

    bb. It dissolves, or diminishes, add HNO_3 to filtrate to distinct acidity, a white ppt................................ **Silver.**

244. To the soln. in which HCl has failed to ppt., or to the filtrate from 243*b*, add H_2S until it smells strongly of the reagent, and warm slightly:

    a. No ppt.=absence of Pb, Bi, Cd, Cu, Hg, Au, Pt, As, Sn, and Sb. Pass to § **248.**

    b. A ppt. is formed:

---

* This is not intended as a complete analytical scheme, but simply as one for the training of the student in the simpler methods of qualitative separations. In preparing the mixtures to be submitted to students the instructor should avoid combinations not provided for in this scheme.

† The acids are determined according to § 126.

DETERMINATION OF THE BASES.

b1. It is yellowish white, and does not disappear on addition of HCl: the ppt. is sulfur and a ferric compound is probably present. Pass to § 248.

b2. It is colored. Saturate the soln. thoroughly with H_2S, with moderate warming and occasional agitation, filter, wash ppt., examine filtrate and washings according to § 248, and ppt. according to § 245.

245. Treat a small portion of the ppt. with $(NH_4)_2S$, with moderate warming, in a test-tube:

a. It dissolves completely = absence of Cd, Pb, Bi, Cu, and Hg. Examine the remainder of the ppt. according to § 246.

b. A part or all remains undissolved: filter, add HCl to a part of the filtrate, and agitate with benzene or petroleum ether:

aa. Only a white ppt. produced by HCl, dissolved by benzene or petroleum ether = absence of As, Sb, Sn, Au, and Pt; examine remainder of ppt. according to § 247.

bb. A colored ppt. remains: warm the entire ppt. produced by H_2S, § 244, with $(NH_4)_2S$ in a flask; filter, after subsidence, wash with H_2O containing a small quantity of $(NH_4)_2S$; examine the insoluble part for Cd, Pb, Bi, Cu, Hg according to § 247, and the solution for As, Sb, Sn, Au, and Pt according to § 246.

246. Add HCl to the solution **245***bb* to acid reaction, agitate with benzene, collect the ppt. on a fil-

DETERMINATION OF THE BASES.

ter, and wash. If this ppt. is brown or black, Sn, Au, or Pt is present; if yellow, As; if orange, Sb. A black or brown ppt. may contain As or Sb, and a yellow or orange traces of Sn, Au, or Pt. Boil ppt. with strong HCl as long as H_2S is given off, dilute slightly, filter:

    a. Filtrate may contain $SbCl_3$ or $SnCl_4$. Place liquid in Pt capsule, immerse rod of Zn in fluid so that it touches Pt outside of the liquid:

        a1. A black stain adherent to Pt, insoluble (after washing) on boiling with HCl................**Antimony.**

        a2. Loose metallic granules, soluble (after washing) on boiling with HCl. Soln. gives ppt. with HgCl.......**Tin.**

    b. Ppt. may contain As_2S_3 (yellow), Au_2S_3, or PtS_2 (black). Shake with $(NH_4)_2CO_3$ soln. (cold), filter.

        b1. Filtrate. Add HCl in excess, a yellow ppt......................**Arsenic.**

        b2. Black ppt. Dissolve in aqua regia, dilute; divide into two parts:

            1. With $SnCl_2$, a purple ppt...**Gold.**

            2. With KCl and alcohol, a yellow, crystalline ppt..........**Platinum.**

247. The ppt. by H_2S, insoluble in $(NH_4)_2S$ from 245*aa* or 245*bb*, which may contain Pb, Bi, Cu, Cd, Hg, is boiled with dilute HNO_3:

    a. A black residue remains, filter, wash, examine filtrate according to 247*b*,

                                Mercury.

    b. Ppt. dissolves completely (except small quantity S), filter, expel most of HNO_3 by

DETERMINATION OF THE BASES.

concentration. To a part of filtrate add excess dil. H_2SO_4, warm, and let stand:

b1. A white ppt., add excess dil. H_2SO_4 to entire filtrate, evaporate to near dryness, dissolve residue in H_2O + trace H_2SO_4, filter, and examine filtrate according to *b2*..................**Lead.**

b2. No ppt. (or filtrate from *b1*). Add NH_4HO in excess to remainder of liquid:
    bb. A white ppt., filter and examine filtrate according to *bb1*,
                                      Bismuth.
    bb1. No ppt. (or filtrate from *bb*). Evaporate nearly to dryness, add H_2O and HCl to faintly acid reaction:
        bbb. A part with $K_4Fe(CN)_6$ gives a brown-red color or ppt.,
                                      Copper.
        bbb1. Remainder, with more HCl and H_2S, a yellow ppt.,
                                    Cadmium.

248. Boil a part of the solution in which neither HCl nor H_2S has caused ppt., or of filtrates from § 244 *b1* and *b2*, add a few gtt. dil. HNO_3, boil, and note color (yellow indicates probable presence of Fe), add NH_4HO just to alkaline reaction, and then $(NH_4)_2S$:

    a. Neither NH_4HO nor $(NH_4)_2S$ causes a ppt. = absence of Fe, Ni, Co, Zn, Mn, Cr, Al. Pass to § 249.

    b. NH_4HO causes a ppt., presence of Fe, Cr, or Al, or one is produced by $(NH_4)_2S$.

DETERMINATION OF THE BASES. 41

Add to entire soln. of which a portion was tested with NH_4HO and $(NH_4)_2S$, first NH_4Cl, then NH_4HO just to alkalinity, then excess $(NH_4)_2S$, agitate, warm, let stand, filter and wash. Examine filtrate according to § **249**.

aa. The ppt. is pure white = absence of Fe, Co, Ni. Dissolve ppt. with small quantity dil. HCl by warming in capsule, boil to expel H_2S, filter if necessary, concentrate to small bulk, add conc. NaHO soln. in excess, and boil:

    aa1. The ppt. caused by NaHO dissolves completely on boiling with excess = absence of Mn and Cr. Presence of Al or Zn. Divide soln. into two parts:

        aaa. Alkaline soln. with H_2S gives a white ppt..........**Zinc**.

        bbb. Add HCl to alkaline liquid to acid reaction, then NH_4HO in slight excess: a white, flocculent ppt.........**Aluminium**.

    aa2. The ppt. does not dissolve completely on boiling with excess NaHO; dilute, filter; test filtrate for Al and Zn as directed in *aaa*, *bbb* above. Wash and dry the ppt.:

        The ppt. is brown or brownish,
                Manganese.

        The soln. in dil. HCl, **248***aa*, was blue violet.........**Chromium**.

bb. The ppt. is not white=it contains

DETERMINATION OF THE BASES. 42

Cr, Mn, Fe, Co, or Ni. Treat the ppt. immediately with dil. HCl:

*bb*1. It dissolves completely (except a little S) = absence of Co and Ni. Boil the soln., add HNO_3, boil again, filter if necessary, concentrate to small bulk, add excess KHO, boil during constant stirring, dilute, filter, wash ppt., examine filtrate, then ppt.:

Filtrate.—A part with H_2S gives a white ppt.............. **Zinc.**
A part with HCl to acidity, then NH_4HO just to alkalinity, gives a white ppt..**Aluminium.**
Ppt.—Dissolve a part in HCl, add $K_4Fe(CN)_6$, a blue ppt.,
Iron.
Dry a part of ppt., fuse with $Na_2CO_3 + KClO_3$, extract with H_2O:
The soln. is yellow,
Chromium.
The soln. is red or green,
Manganese.
Dissolve a part of ppt. in HCl, evaporate to small bulk, add $NaC_2H_3O_2$, treat with H_2S, a white ppt................**Zinc.**

*bb*2. It leaves a black residue: filter, wash; examine filtrate as in *bb*1. Dry and ignite the filter and residue, warm with HCl and a little HNO_3, add H_2O, then NH_4HO in

slight excess, filter, evaporate the filtrate, and ignite the residue.
Heat a part of the residue with borax in the inner and outer blowpipe flame:
The bead in the oxidizing flame is violet when hot, red-brown when cold, and is gray and opaque in the reduction flame, **Nickel.**
The bead is blue in either flame, hot or cold............**Cobalt.**

249. Add to a portion of the liquid in which neither HCl, H_2S, NH_4HO nor $(NH_4)_2S$ has caused a ppt., or of the filtrate from § 248b, first NH_4Cl, then NH_4HO and $(NH_4)_2CO_3$, and warm some time gently:

a. No ppt. is produced = absence of Ca, Ba, or Sr; examine the remainder of the liquid according to § **250.**

b. A ppt. is produced: treat the remainder of the liquid with NH_4Cl, NH_4HO, and $(NH_4)_2CO_3$, warm gently, filter, examine the filtrate according to § **250.** Wash the ppt. with H_2O containing NH_4HO, dissolve in $C_2H_4O_2$, and add K_2CrO_4 in excess:

$b1$. A yellow ppt., filter and examine filtrate according to $b2$..........**Barium.**

$b2$. To a small portion of the filtrate add $CaSO_4$ and warm gently:

$bb1$. A ppt. is formed, filter, examine filtrate according to $bb2$, the dried ppt. + HCl on Pt wire colors Bunsen flame crimson,
Strontium.

DETERMINATION OF THE BASES. 44

$bb2$. Add to filtrate from $bb1$, or to a portion of liquid from b if $CaSO_4$ caused no ppt. in $b2$, NH_4HO and $(NH_4)_2C_2O_4$: a white ppt.,
Calcium.

250. To a portion of the liquid from § 249a, or of the filtrate from § 249b, add NH_4Cl (if not already added), then NH_4HO and HNa_2PO_4, rub inside of test-tube gently with glass rod, and let stand:

    a. A white ppt., crystalline, and formed if in small quantity where test-tube has been rubbed .... **Magnesium.**

    b. No ppt. is produced, pass to § 251.

251. A. Magnesium was absent in § 250, evaporate another portion of the liquid § 249a or § 249b to dryness and ignite gently:

    a. No residue remains = absence of K or Na, proceed to § 253.

    b. A residue remains = presence of K or Na, examine residue according to § 252.

B. Magnesium was present in § 250; evaporate another portion of the liquid § 249a or § 249b to dryness, ignite until NH_4 salts are expelled, warm residue with H_2O, add $BaCl_2$ so long as it produces a ppt., then BaH_2O_2 during heating to distinct alkalinity; boil, filter, add $(NH_4)_2CO_3 + NH_4HO$ in slight excess to filtrate, warm gently some time, filter, evaporate, and ignite residue gently until NH_4 salts are expelled:

    a. No residue remains = absence of K or Na; pass to § 253.

    b. A residue remains = presence of K or Na; examine residue according to § 252.

252. Dissolve residue from 251Ab or 251Bb in

a little H_2O, add a little NH_4HO, then $(NH_4)_2CO_3$, warm some time, filter if necessary, evaporate clear liquid or filtrate to dryness, ignite gently to expel NH_4 salts, dissolve residue in small quantity H_2O; divide clear liquid into two parts:

    a. Add to half the liquid in a porcelain capsule $PtCl_4$; a yellow, crystalline ppt.,
Potassium.

    b. To other half of liquid (neutralized, if acid, with Na_2CO_3) in a watch-glass add a freshly prepared and filtered soln. of K_2H_2-Sb_2O_7; a white, crystalline ppt....**Sodium.**

253. To a portion of the original soln. or solid add excess of CaH_2O_2, and H_2O if necessary, and boil; steam smells of NH_3, blues red litmus, and gives white cloud from glass rod moistened with HCl,
Ammonium.

QUALITATIVE ANALYSIS OF URINE.

PHYSICAL CHARACTERS.

Quantity.

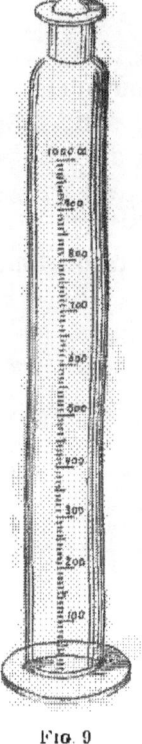

Fig. 9

254. Collect all urine passed by the patient during twenty-four hours, and measure in a cylindrical graduate (Fig. 9) divided into cubic centimetres.

Normal = 1,000 to 1,500 cc.

All examinations of urine should be made with samples of the mixed urine of twenty-four hours, unless otherwise directed.

Color.

255. Put 100 cc. urine (filtered if cloudy) into a beaker of 6 to 7 centimetres diameter; look through it at the light from a window, and compare the color observed with the color plate. (See plate.) Record this, by using the numbers of the colored squares, as *free color*. Add 5 cc. HCl to the urine; stir, let stand four hours, compare color as before, and record as *total color*.

Odor.

256. Note whether the odor is natural or "urinous," or "ammoniacal," "like violets," or otherwise peculiar.

Reaction.

257. If the reaction be found to be alkaline, it remains to determine whether the alkalinity is due to fixed or volatile alkali, to carbonates or phosphates. These determinations must be made with the urine so soon as possible after it has been voided, and, preferably, with the morning urine.

258. Moisten one-half of a piece of red litmus paper with the urine, and hang it up to dry. If, after drying, the paper retain its blue color, the alkalinity is due to fixed alkali; but if the paper return to its original red, to volatile alkali (ammonia).

To obtain reliable results, the paper must be dried in a position where it is not exposed to the fumes coming from bottles containing NH_4HO, HCl, or HNO_3, or to other acid or ammoniacal vapors.

259. To a portion of the urine in a test-tube add a slight excess of HCl, and warm, if necessary. If effervescence ensue, the alkalinity is due to carbonates; if not, to phosphates.

If volatile alkali be found in 258, and carbonate in 259, the urine contains ammonium carbonate.

Specific Gravity.

260. Test the urinometer (which should not be smaller than 12 centimetres in length, and divided into single degrees) with the solutions of known specific gravity furnished in the laboratory for that purpose, making the readings as directed in § 261, and note the error in different parts of the scale. The differences from the true readings are to be noted on the box, and added or subtracted, as the error is minus or plus, in all subsequent readings.

261. To use the urinometer: The cylinder should

be of the shape shown in Fig. 10, without pouring-lip, of such depth that the urinometer may be completely immersed, and of a diameter double that of the wide part of the urinometer.

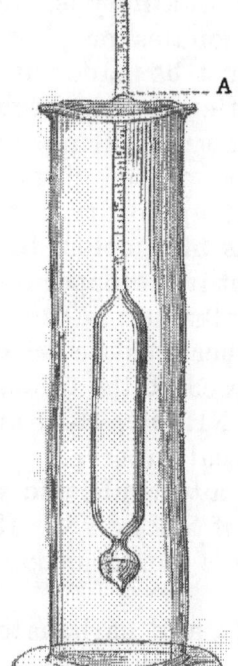

Fig. 10.

Hold the cylinder in an inclined position, and pour into it urine to within 2 centimetres of the top. Set it upright, float the urinometer in the urine, and add more urine until the level "heaps" above the rim of the cylinder. Now bring the eye to about the level of the top of the cylinder, and, seeing that the urinometer does not touch the wall of the cylinder, read off the specific gravity at the *highest* point where the liquid, drawn up by capillary attraction, cuts the graduation of the urinometer (A, Fig. 10).

262. The temperature at which the gravity should be determined is 60° F (= 15°.4 Cent.). If the urine be of a different temperature, cool it by immersing the vessel in cold water, or warm it until 60° is reached.

Corrections for variations of temperature cannot be accurately made in the case of a liquid of such complex and varying composition as the urine.

CHEMICAL CHARACTERS—COMPOSITION.

Normal Constituents.

N. B.—Obviously a qualitative examination of the urine for its normal constituents is never practised by the physician. The student is required to test for the more important of these substances, to afford practice in the methods of manipulation and observation.

Normal Urine Contains:

Water, Sodium,
Chlorids, Potassium,
Sulfates, Calcium,
Phosphates, Magnesium,
Urea,
Uric acid,
Urates,
Hippuric acid,
Creatinin,
Coloring matters, etc., etc.

Urea.

263. To a moderately concentrated cold soln. of urea in a watch-glass add colorless HNO_3 in equal volume — immediately, or after a few moments, crystals of nitrate of urea (Fig. 11) separate.

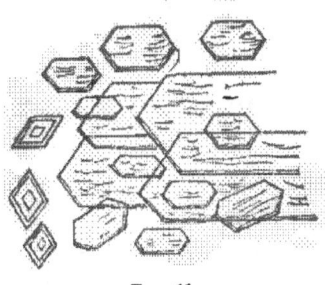

Fig. 11.

264. To a few drops of a soln. of urea upon a watch-glass add a few gtt. of Millon's reagent,* and heat—a yellow color, changing to

---

* Made by dissolving 1 pt. Hg in 2 pts. strong HNO_3 over the water-bath, diluting with 2 pts. H_2O, and decanting after four hours.

red, is produced. A somewhat similar appearance is produced with albumins.

265. Heat a fragment of urea in a dry test-tube until, after having fused, it is converted into an opaque, white solid; let cool; add about 1 cent. KHO and 2 gtt. of a very dilute soln. $CuSO_4$,—a pale rose-red color. This test, known as the "*biuret reaction*," produces a similar appearance with peptones. See § 281.

Uric Acid.

266. Moisten the solid in a porcelain capsule with a few gtt. HNO_3; heat on the water-bath until dry; cool; add NH_4HO—a brilliant red color appears, which fades after a few moments. This is known as the "*murexid test*."

Abnormal Constituents.
PROTEIDS — ALBUMINOIDS.

Before testing for albuminoids, the urine must be separated from all solid particles, must be rendered perfectly clear and transparent, this is accomplished by filtration.

267. It frequently happens that urine does not yield a clear filtrate by simple filtration. When this is the case, add to the turbid filtrate enough KHO to communicate a distinctly alkaline reaction, and a few gtt. of magnesia mixture, warm slightly, and filter again through a fresh filter.

Albumin.

268. *Heller's test.*—Put about 2 cent. HNO_3 into a test-tube. Fill a pipette with the filtered urine. Hold the test-tube at a small angle to the horizontal, and allow the urine to flow *slowly* from the pipette (whose upper end has been roughened by the file) upon the surface of the nitric acid (Fig. 12). Remove the pipette, turn the test-tube cautiously into

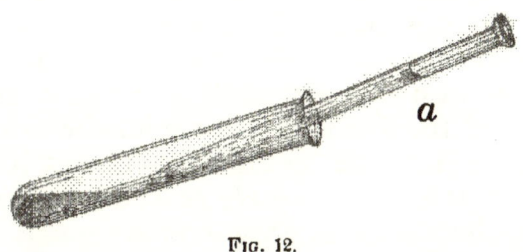

Fig. 12.

the vertical position, and examine the point of junction of the two liquids. In the presence of albumin a milky zone, whose upper and lower borders are both sharply defined, is seen *at* the point of junction of the acid and urine (Fig 13, *a*). If no reaction be observed, set the tube aside and examine it again in half an hour.

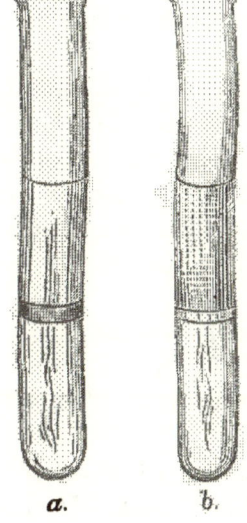

Fig. 13.

269. Repeat the testing, as in § 268, with a non-albuminous urine. A band of deeper coloration is observed at the point of junction of the two liquids: this is not to be confounded with the milky zone observed with albuminous urine.

270. Repeat the testing, as in § 268, using a urine containing an excess of urates, but no albumin. A white zone is observed *above* the point of junction of the liquids, whose lower border may be sharply defined, but whose upper border fades off gradually into the

ALBUMIN. 52

layer of urine, the whole of which may become turbid (Fig 13, *b*).

271. *Heat and Nitric Acid test.*—Determine the reaction of the urine. If it be alkaline, add acetic acid cautiously until it shows a *faintly* acid reaction with blue litmus paper. Fill a test-tube to within 2-3 cent. of the top with the acidulated urine, and, holding the test-tube by the bottom, heat the upper portion of the liquid *nearly to boiling*. An opalescence, cloudiness, or coagulum is formed, according to the amount of albumin present. Now add slowly 5 to 10 gtt. of concentrated HNO_3; the ppt. does not diminish (it may increase) in amount.

272. Apply heat, as in § 271, to a sample of the alkaline albuminous urine, without acidulating. No reaction is observed.

273. Apply heat, as in § 271, to another sample of the urine, to which an excess of acetic acid has been added. No reaction is observed.

274. Apply the test, as directed in § 271 (but do not acidify), to a sample of urine containing no albumin, but containing an excess of earthy phosphates. An appearance similar to that observed in the case of the albuminous urine is obtained; but on addition of HNO_3 the ppt. redissolves and the liquid becomes transparent.

275. If the urine, when heated, becomes cloudy, and again clears on addition of HNO_3 in the amount mentioned in § 271, it contains an amount of earthy phosphates in excess of the normal.

276. *Picric Acid test.*—Float some of the *clear* urine on acetic acid as in Heller's test. If any cloudiness be observed at the junction of the two liquids, treat a larger quantity of the urine with acetic acid to acid reaction, and filter. Pour about 7 cent. of the *clear* filtrate, or of the *clear* urine, which gives no cloudiness when floated on acetic acid, into a test-tube; float upon its surface about 2 cent. of a saturated solution of picric acid, and warm the point where the two liquids come together. A cloudiness at this point, which does not disappear when heat is applied, is evidence of the presence of albumin.

A cloudiness which *does* disappear on the application of heat may be produced by alkaloids, urates, etc.

Paraglobulin.

277. Dilute the filtered urine with water to sp. gr. 1.002. Float on the surface dilute acetic acid (1 to 10); a cloudy zone is formed in the presence of paraglobulin in large amount. If no cloudiness be observed after half an hour, pass through the liquid a slow current of carbon dioxid. A cloudiness indicates the presence of paraglobulin.

Mucin.

278. Pour about 2 cent. of acetic acid into a test-tube, and float the clear urine upon its surface. A cloud, which usually appears only after standing for a time, just above the line of contact of the liquids, shows the presence of mucin, provided it does not disappear on the application of heat.

Peptone.

279. Add soln. of neutral lead acetate to 500 cc. urine until the ppt. no longer increases; filter. To the filtrate add acetic acid and a few gtt. of potassium ferrocyanid soln.; if any cloudiness be pro-

duced, continue the addition of ferrocyanid soln. until the precipitate no longer increases, and filter.

280. To a portion of the last filtrate obtained as in § 279, add one-fifth its bulk of acetic acid and then an acid soln. of sodium phosphotungstate.* A cloudiness immediately, or after a few moments, indicates the presence of peptone.

281. To the remainder of the filtrate, § 279, add half its volume of strong HCl, and then phosphotungstate soln. to complete precipitation. Collect the ppt. on a filter as rapidly as possible, wash with 5% H_2SO_4 until the filtrate is colorless. Transfer the ppt. to a capsule and mix it thoroughly with powdered barium hydroxid; add a little H_2O; warm fifteen minutes on the water-bath, and filter. Add to a portion of the filtrate in a test-tube KHO soln. to strongly alkaline reaction, and then 1 gtt. of a dil. soln. of $CuSO_4$. A reddish-violet color indicates the presence of peptone. See § 265.

Glucose—Diabetic Sugar.†

282. Test the urine for albumin; if it be present, remove it as follows before testing for sugar: Heat the urine in a beaker. and, when it begins to boil, add 2 gtt. acetic acid, largely diluted with water, and boil gently for half an hour, or until the albu-

---

* The phosphotungstate soln. is made by adding phosphoric acid to a boiling soln. of sodium tungstate to acid reaction, cooling, adding acetic acid to strongly acid reaction, and filtering after twenty-four hours.

† Glucose is considered as an abnormal constituent of the urine for clinical convenience. Strictly speaking, it is a normal constituent. It is constantly present, but in such minute quantity that the tests, as usually applied, fail to reveal its presence so long as the quantity remains within the normal limits.

GLUCOSE.

min, which was at first disseminated throughout the liquid, has separated in flocks. Filter, and apply the following tests to the filtrate:

283. Urine containing sugar is *usually* of high sp. gr., pale in color, abundant in quantity, and sometimes has a sweetish odor.

284. *Moore's test.*—To the urine in two test-tubes add one-half bulk of KHO. Boil the contents of one tube for about a minute, and then compare its color with that of the other tube. A darkening of the boiled sample indicates the presence of sugar.

N. B.—In boiling a liquid in a test-tube, hold the tube by its upper end, between the thumb and forefinger, the mouth pointing over the forefinger and away from the person Hold the bottom of the tube in the flame until small bubbles begin to rise through the liquid; then, and so long as the heating continues, prevent "bumping" of the contents by an oscillation of the tube, produced by rapidly alternating slight motions of pronation and supination of the hand.

In cases where prolonged boiling is necessary, the tube may be held in a wooden clamp, or by passing around its upper part a folded strip of strong paper, whose ends are then grasped between the thumb and forefinger.

285. *Trommer's test.*—To the urine in a test-tube add 2 gtt. of a saturated soln. of $CuSO_4$ and a volume of KHO soln. equal to half that of the urine. Observe that the liquid is blue and transparent. Heat until the liquid *begins* to boil. The formation of a yellow or red ppt. indicates the presence of glucose.

286. Apply the test as described in § 285, using a

urine containing a large amount of sugar. The
liquid changes in color from blue to yellow, but no
ppt. is produced.

287. Repeat the testing of the highly saccharine
urine, adding 6 gtt. in place of 2 gtt. $CuSO_4$ soln.,
and allow the liquid to stand after boiling. The
yellow or red ppt. is produced.

288. Repeat the test with the urine used in § 285,
adding 6 gtt. $CuSO_4$ soln., and boiling for a longer
time. A black or dark colored ppt. is produced.

N.B.—Trommer's test only shows that sugar is
present when a *distinct yellow or red ppt.* is formed.
A mere change of color, or the formation of a ppt.
different from that described, is not sufficient evidence of the presence of sugar. Therefore, in apply-
ing this test in practice, use only a small quantity
of $CuSO_4$ soln. at first, and if in a first testing a
change of color be observed, but no ppt., make a
second testing, using an increased amount of $CuSO_4$.

289. *Boettger's test.*—Render the urine strongly
alkaline by dissolving in it powdered Na_2CO_3. Put
into two test-tubes about 3 cent. of the alkaline
urine. To one test-tube add a very minute quantity
of powdered subnitrate of bismuth, to the other as
much powdered litharge. Boil the contents of the
two tubes. If sugar be present, the bismuth powder becomes first gray and then black. The litharge
is not blackened.

290. Repeat the test as in § 289 with a urine
containing a sulfid or an organic compound containing sulfur, but no sugar. Both subnitrate and
litharge are blackened.

291. *Mulder-Neubauer test.*—Dissolve in 2 cent.
of the saccharine urine in a test-tube enough pow-

GLUCOSE. 57

dered Na_2CO_3 to give it a strongly alkaline reaction, and then enough solution of indigo-carmin to communicate a distinctly blue color, but no more. Heat the liquid to boiling with as little agitation as possible. The color changes from blue to green, to wine-red, to yellow. Allow the contents of the tube to cool. Close the opening of the tube with the thumb, and agitate; the color changes back through wine-red and green to blue.

292. *Fermentation test.*—Take three beakers of about 70 cc. capacity, and label them A, B, and C. Fill A with the urine to be tested, B with a solution of glucose, and C with water. Put into each beaker some brewer's yeast, or some compressed yeast, and stir well. Fill a test-tube completely full from A. Close the opening of the tube with a cork of suitable size fastened on the short limb of a wire bent at right angles, in such a way that no air bubbles are enclosed. Immerse the end of the tube with the cork into the liquid in A, and remove the cork by means of the wire, taking care that no air enters the tube. Reverse test-tubes similarly filled from B and C in each of those beakers. Set the three beakers and tubes in a place whose temperature is about 25° (77° Fahr.), and after six hours observe whether gas have collected in any of the tubes. If the test-tubes A and B contain gas above the liquid, and C do not, the urine contains sugar. If A and C do not contain gas, and B do, the urine does not contain sugar. Under any other circumstances the yeast is unfit for use.

The purpose of A is to test the urine; that of B and C, to guard against sources of error from the yeast itself.

293. *Fehling's test.*—Put about 2 cent. of Fehling's solution (see § 328) into a test-tube, and heat it to boiling. Examine the liquid carefully—standing with your back to the light, and, if possible, holding the tube in the direct rays of the sun—for any red specks or reddish reflections, which appear usually at the lower, curved part of the tube. If any red color be observed, the test solution has deteriorated and must be replaced by some which has been freshly mixed.

294. If the test solution have been found to be in proper condition, add to it 2 to 3 gtt. of the urine to be tested, and boil again. If no red color be now observed, add a further quantity of urine and boil again. Continue this alternate addition of urine and boiling until a red or yellow ppt. is formed—in which case sugar is present—or until a bulk of urine equal to that of the test solution used has been added, without the appearance of a red ppt.—in which case sugar is absent.

N B.—Fehling's solution is recommended as affording the most manageable and reliable test for sugar, provided the precautions mentioned in §§ 293 and 282 are observed. When the amount of sugar present is very small, the liquid retains its blue color; but when it is poured out of the tube, a red film is seen attached to the glass. If the quantity of sugar be great, the copper is completely precipitated and the liquid decolorized.

Test-tubes which have been used for Fehling's and Trommer's tests may be cleaned with a little HNO_3.

Blood.

295 If the urine be alkaline, render it *faintly*

acid with acetic acid. Heat to near boiling. The urine becomes lighter in color, and a dark-colored coagulum is formed.

296. Add KHO to distinct alkaline reaction; heat nearly to boiling (do not boil). A red ppt. is produced.

297. To a few drops of the urine in a test-tube add a drop of freshly prepared tincture of guaiacum and a little ozonic ether (ether to which oxygenated water has been added), and agitate. The ether, which rises to the surface, is blue.

Shake together oil of turpentine and freshly prepared tincture of guaiac, add the urine in volume equal to that of the resulting emulsion. shake gently, and allow to separate: a blue or greenish-blue color of the upper layer indicates the presence of blood.

Bile.

Biliary Salts.

298. *Pettenkofer's Reaction.*—This test, although very useful with pure solutions of the biliary acids, cannot be applied to the urine directly; a process of purification is therefore necessary, and is performed as follows: About 50–100 cc. of the urine are evaporated to dryness over the water-bath. The residue is extracted with strong alcohol, 5 cc.; the alcoholic solution is filtered and mixed with 50 cc. anhydrous ether. The ppt. formed is collected on a small filter, and, after having been washed with ether, is dissolved in 1 to 2 cc. H_2O. To the aqueous solution so obtained Pettenkofer's test is applied as directed in § 299.

299. To the liquid obtained according to § 298 add

1 gtt. of a solution of cane-sugar (1:3); hold the tube in an inclined position, and add H_2SO_4 in such a way that it forms a layer below the aqueous liquid. In the presence of biliary acids the liquid becomes turbid, and immediately, or after a time, a purple-red band is formed at the junction of the two strata, which gradually diffuse into one another, forming, after four to five hours, a homogeneous dark-purple liquid. The acid and liquid above must not be mixed.

300. Repeat the test, as in § 299, with urine containing albumin but no biliary salts. The same reaction is produced.

301. Repeat the test, as in § 299, with urine containing morphin but no biliary salts. The same reaction is produced.

Repeat the test, as in § 299, with normal urine. An appearance frequently results which cannot be distinguished from that produced with urine containing biliary acids.

302. *Oliver's Peptone test.*—The reagent required is made by dissolving 2 gm. of pulverized peptone (Savory & Moore) and 0.25 gm. salicylic acid in 250 cc. of H_2O, and adding 2 cc. acetic acid. Filter till perfectly clear.

Dilute the urine to sp. gr. 1.008; pour some into a test-tube, and float upon its surface some of the reagent. An immediate cloudiness at the line of junction of the liquids indicates the presence of biliary salts.

Biliary Pigments.

303. Urine containing biliary pigments is always dark in color.

304. Gmelin's test.—Pour 3 cent. HNO_3 into a test-tube, add a piece of wood (1 cent. of the butt end of a match), and heat until the acid assumes a yellow color. Pour off the acid into another test-tube, and cool it by immersing the tube into cold H_2O. When the acid is cold, float about 3 cent. of the urine to be tested upon its surface from a pipette. If biliary pigments be present, a green band is formed at the junction of the two liquids, which gradually rises higher and higher, and is succeeded from below by blue, reddish-violet, and yellow. The green color is much more distinctly marked than the others.

305. Shake the urine with ether. On standing, the ether separates as a *yellow* layer over the urine. Pour off the ether and float it on the surface of dilute bromin water in another test-tube. The ether gradually changes in color from yellow to blue.

QUANTITATIVE ANALYSIS OF URINE.

Reaction.

Alkalimetry and Acidimetry.

306. To determine the degree of acidity or alkalinity of the urine, solutions containing known quantities of oxalic acid and of caustic soda are required

307. Weigh out 6.3 gm. of pure, crystallized oxalic acid ($C_2O_4H_2 + 2Aq = 126$). Transfer it without loss to the measuring cylinder (Fig. 9, p. 46); add H_2O to the 1,000 cc. mark, and agitate until solution is complete. The liquid so obtained is a "*Decinormal solution of oxalic acid*," each cc. of which contains 0.0063 gm. of oxalic acid, equivalent to 0.004 gm. NaHO.

308. Weigh out 4.5 gm. of caustic soda. Dissolve in 60 cc. H_2O; add a lump of quicklime; boil about fifteen minutes; filter into the measuring cylinder; dilute to 900 cc. with H_2O, and mix.

Measure off 10 cc. of the decinormal oxalic acid solution with a pipette (Fig. 14); transfer it to a small beaker, and add to it 2 gtt. of an alcoholic solution of phenolphthaleïn (1 gm. in 100 cc.). Fill a burette (Fig. 15) with the soda solution to the 0 mark. Add the alkaline solution to the liquid in the beaker until the latter remains *faintly* red after stirring. Read the number of cc. of alkaline solution used from the graduation of the burette. This, multiplied by 100, gives the number of cc. of the solution containing 4.0 gm. of NaHO. Remove soda solution from the mixing cylinder until there remain exactly the number of cc. containing 4.0 gm. NaHO; add H_2O to the 1,000 cc. mark, and mix.

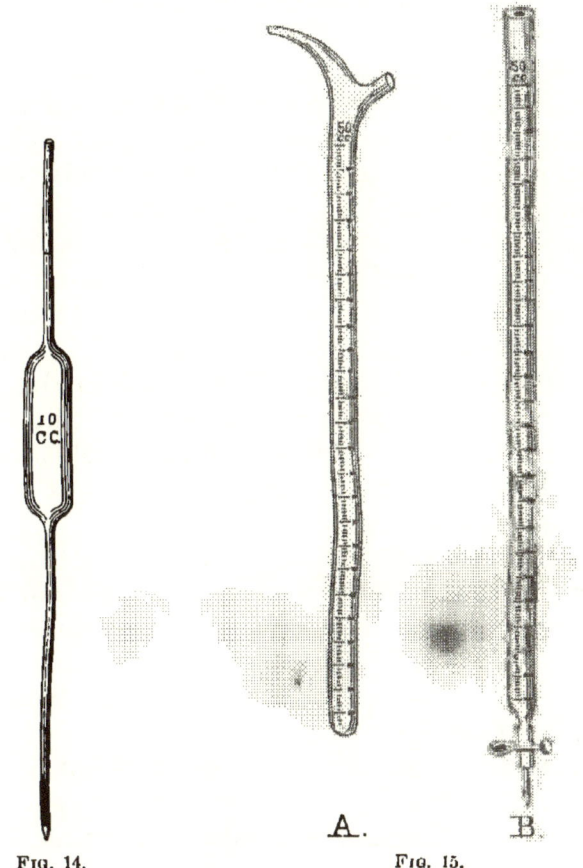

Fig. 14.   Fig. 15.

The solution so obtained is a "*Decinormal solution of caustic soda,*" each cc. of which contains 0.004 gm. NaHO, equivalent to $0.0063C_2O_4H_2 + 2Aq$. The acid and alkaline solutions, therefore, neutralize each other, volume for volume.

The alkaline solution must be kept in glass-stoppered bottles, the stoppers and necks of which have been coated with a mixture of equal parts of vaselin and paraffin, and must be exposed to the air as little as possible.

309. To determine the degree of acidity in the urine, place two portions of 50 cc. each in two beakers, and add to each 4 gtt. phenolphthaleïn solution. Fill a burette to the 0 mark with the decinormal soda solution. Add portions of the alkaline solution to the contents of one of the beakers until a red color is produced, which persists on stirring. Fill the burette again to the 0 mark, and from it add 1 cc. less soda solution to the second beaker than was added to the first. The liquid in the second beaker should be yellow, without any tinge of red. Now continue the addition of soda solution to the second beaker, drop by drop, until a *faint red tinge* persists on stirring.

The number of cc. of decinormal soda solution used (the last burette reading) multiplied by 0.0063 gives the acidity of 50 cc. in grams of oxalic acid; from which the total acidity is determined by multiplying by the quantity of urine in twenty-four hours and dividing by 50.

Example. Quantity of urine in 24 hours = 1,350 cc.

Decinormal soda solution used = 14.6 cc.

$14.6 \times 0.0063 = 0.09198 =$ acidity of 50 cc. urine.

$\dfrac{0.09198 \times 1,350}{50} = 2.48 =$ acidity of 24 hours in grams of oxalic acid.

310. To determine the degree of alkalinity, proceed as in § 309, using the decinormal oxalic acid solution in place of the soda solution in the burette, and adding the acid solution to the contents of the second beaker until the red color *just* disappears. The number of cc. of acid solution used multiplied by 0.004 gives the alkalinity of 50 cc.; from which the total alkalinity is calculated as in § 309.

Example. Quantity of urine in 24 hours = 1,350 cc.

Decinormal oxalic acid soln. used = 7.4 cc.

$7.4 \times 0.004 = 0.0296$ = alkalinity of 50 cc. urine.

$\dfrac{0.0296 \times 1,350}{50} = 0.80$ = alkalinity of 24 hours in grams of caustic soda.

311. The normal acidity of twenty-four hours of the urine is equal to two to four grams of oxalic acid.

Chlorids.

312. The solutions required are: 1. *A standard solution of silver nitrate*, made by dissolving 29.075 gm. of pure, fused, and recrystallized $AgNO_3$ in 1,000 cc. H_2O. This solution must be kept in bottles of amber glass. 2. *A solution of neutral potassium chromate;* 10 gm. to 100 cc. H_2O.

313. To conduct the determination, 5 cc. of urine are placed in a platinum basin, 2 gm. of $NaNO_3$ (free from chlorid) are added. The whole is evaporated to dryness over the water-bath, and the residue gradually heated until a colorless fused mass remains. This residue, after cooling, is dissolved in H_2O, the soln. transferred to a small beaker, treated with pure, dil. HNO_3 to faintly acid reaction, and neutralized with powdered $CaCO_3$; 2 gtt. of the chromate soln. are now added, and finally the silver soln. from a burette (previously filled with $AgNO_3$ soln. to the 0 mark), during constant stirring of the contents of the beaker, until a faint reddish tinge remains permanent. Each cc. of the $AgNO_3$ soln. used represents 0.01 gm. NaCl (or 0.0607 gm. Cl) in 5 cc. urine; from which the NaCl in twenty-four hours is calculated.

Example. Urine in 24 hours = 1,260 cc.
Silver soln. used = 6.7 cc.

$$\frac{0.01 \times 6.7}{5} \times 1{,}260 = 16.88 \text{ gm. NaCl in 24 hours.}$$

N. B.—This process cannot be used during administration of bromids or iodids.

314. The amount of Cl voided by a normal male adult, upon normal diet, is about 10 grams in twenty-four hours, equivalent to 16.5 gm. NaCl.

Phosphates.

315. The solutions required are: 1. *A standard solution of disodic phosphate,* made by dissolving 10.085 gm. of crystallized, non-effloresced disodic phosphate ($Na_2HPO_4 + 12Aq.$) in H_2O, and diluting the solution to 1 litre. Fifty cc. of this soln. contain 0.1 gm. phosphoric anhydrid, P_2O_5. 2. *An acid solution of sodium acetate,* made by dissolving 100 gm. $NaC_2H_3O_2 + 3Aq.$ in 100 cc. H_2O, adding 100 cc. glacial $HC_2H_3O_2$, and diluting with H_2O to 1,000 cc. 3. *A solution of potassium ferrocyanid,* 10 gm. in 100 cc. H_2O. 4. *A standard solution* of uranic acetate. To obtain this soln., a soln. of approximate strength is first made by dissolving 33 gm. of yellow uranic oxid in glacial acetic acid, and diluting with H_2O to 900 cc. in the mixing cylinder. Solution No.

PHOSPHATES. 67

1 serves to determine the true strength of this soln., as follows: 50 cc. of soln. 1 are placed in a beaker, and 5 cc. of soln. 2 are added. The mixture is heated on the water-bath, and the uranium soln. gradually added from a burette until a drop of the liquid, taken from the beaker on a stirring-rod, produces a brown color when brought in contact with a drop of soln. 3. At this point the reading of the burette, which indicates the number of cc. of the uranium soln. corresponding to 0.1 gm. P_2O_5, is taken. This reading multiplied by 50 gives the number of cc. uranium soln. equivalent to 5 gm. P_2O_5. Remove uranium soln. from the mixing cylinder until there remain the number of cc. which have been found to be equivalent to 5 gm P_2O_5; add H_2O to the 1,000 cc. mark, and mix. The uranium solution so standardized is of such strength that each cc. is equivalent to 0.005 gm. P_2O_5.

316. To determine the *total phosphoric anhydrid* in the urine, 50 cc. are placed in a beaker, 5 cc. sodium acetate soln. are added, and the mixture heated on the water-bath. When warm, the standard uranium soln. is added from a burette until a drop, removed from the beaker with a stirring-rod, produces a faint brown tinge when brought in contact with a drop of ferrocyanid soln. The burette reading taken at this point and multiplied by 0.005 gives the amount of P_2O_5 in 50 cc. urine; and this, multiplied by $\frac{1}{50}$ the amount of urine eliminated in twenty-four hours, gives the daily elimination in grams of P_2O_5.

Example. Urine in 24 hours = 1,180 cc.
Uranium solution used = 24.3 cc.
24.3 × 0.005 = 0.1215.

$$\frac{1,180 \times 0.1215}{50} = 2.87 = \text{grams } P_2O_5 \text{ in 24 hours.}$$

SULFATES. 68

317. To determine the *phosphoric anhydrid corresponding to earthy phosphates*, 100 cc. of the urine are rendered alkaline with NH_4HO, and set aside for twelve hours. Collect the ppt. on a filter, wash it with dilute ammonium hydroxid soln. (1 : 3). Perforate the point of the filter, and wash the ppt. into a small beaker; dissolve in as little acetic acid as possible; make up the solution to about 50 cc. with H_2O, add 5 cc. sodium acetate soln., and titrate as in § 316.

N. B.—In standardizing (§ 315) the uranium soln., and in using it (§§ 316, 317), time will be saved by taking two quantities of 50 cc. each of the phosphate soln. or urine. Make an approximate determination with one beaker, by adding to it 15 cc. of the uranium soln., and then further quantities of 2 cc. each until the red color is obtained with ferrocyanid. Then add to the second beaker an amount of uranium soln. equal to that which last failed to respond to the ferrocyanid soln. in the first sample, and continue the addition of uranium soln., drop by drop, until the final reaction is obtained.

318. The normal amount of phosphoric anhydrid in twenty-four hours is 2.5 to 3 5 gm., of which 0.8 to 1.2 gm. are in combination as earthy phosphates, and 1.7 to 2.3 as alkaline phosphates.

Sulfates.

319. To 100 cc. of the urine add 5 cc. HCl; heat to near boiling; add $BaCl_2$ soln. in slight excess; let the beaker containing the mixture stand on the water-bath until the ppt. has subsided; decant the clear liquid through a small filter without disturbing the ppt.; add hot water to the beaker; let the ppt. settle again, decant as before, and continue this washing by decantation until a portion of the filtrate no longer becomes cloudy on addition of dil-H_2SO_4. Transfer the ppt. to the filter by the aid of the wash-bottle (Fig. 5, p 7), and dry in the water-oven. Burn the filter in a weighed platinum crucible until white. Weigh the crucible, ash, and $BaSO_4$, and from this weight subtract that of the crucible and filter-ash. The difference, multiplied by 0.421, is the weight of sulfuric acid, H_2SO_4, in 100 cc. urine; and this, multiplied by $\frac{1}{100}$ of the quantity in twenty-four hours, is the amount of H_2SO_4 eliminated in twenty-four hours.

Example. Quantity of urine in 24 hours = 1,320 cc.
Weight of platinum crucible, filter-ash,
and $BaSO_4$ = 17.8932
" " " " and filter-ash = 17.4863

Weight of $BaSO_4$ = 0.4069
0.4069 × 0.421 = 0.1713 = grams H_2SO_4 in 100 cc.
0.1713 × 13.20 = 2.26 = grams H_2SO_4 in 24 hours.

320. The normal daily elimination of H_2SO_4 is from 2 to 2.5 gm.

Urea.

321. Urine containing an excess of urea has a high specific gravity, while that which is deficient in urea is of lower specific gravity than normal.

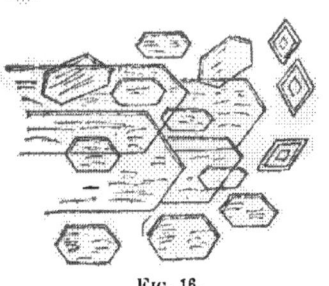

Fig. 16.

322. Take two watch-glasses. Into one put 5 gtt. of the urine, into the other 10 gtt. Evaporate the latter over the water-bath until it has been reduced to the volume of the former. Cool

the contents of both watch glasses to about 15° (59°
Fahr.), and add to each 3 gtt. of cold, colorless,
concentrated HNO_3. If, after a few moments, crystals of urea nitrate (Fig. 16) appear in both watch-
glasses, the urine contains an excess of urea; if
crystals do not form in either watch-glass, the proportion of urea is deficient; while if crystals appear
in one and not in the other, the amount of urea is
about normal.

This method is only capable of showing roughly
an increase or a diminution in the proportion of
urea. Two precautions are to be observed in its
use: 1. The *amorphous* deposit produced in albuminous urine is not to be mistaken for the *crystalline*
urea nitrate. 2. The process can be applied as described above only when the quantity of urine in
twenty-four hours is about normal. If it be greater
or less than normal, a modification is necessary. If,
for instance, the quantity of urine in twenty-four
hours be half the normal, two samples of 5 gtt. each
are to be taken, one of which is to be diluted with 5
gtt. H_2O. If the quantity in twenty-four hours be
double the normal, two samples are to be taken, one
of 10 gtt., the other of 20 gtt., and both reduced to 5
gtt. by evaporation.

323. *Fowler's method.*—Determine the sp. gr. of
the urine and the sp. gr. of some liq. sodæ chlori-
natæ (Squibb) at the same temperature. Mix one
volume of the urine with seven volumes of the liq.
sod. chlor. After the violence of the reaction has
subsided, shake the mixture from time to time during an hour. Determine the sp. gr. of the mixture
at the same temperature at which the former obser-
vations were made. Add once the sp. gr. of the

URIC ACID. 71

urine to seven times the sp. gr. of the liq. sod. chlor., and divide the sum by eight. From the quotient so obtained subtract the sp. gr. of the mixture after decomposition, and multiply the difference by 0.7791. The product is the amount of urea in grams in 100 cc.; from which the elimination in twenty-four hours is obtained by multiplying by $\frac{1}{100}$ of the quantity in twenty-four hours.

Example. Quantity of urine in 24 hours = 1,240 cc.
Specific gravity of liq. sod. chlor. = 1,042
" " " urine = 1,020
.. " " mixture = 1,036.2

$$\frac{1,042 \times 7 + 1,020}{8} = 1,039.25. \quad 1,0393 - 1,036.2 =$$

3.1. 0.7791 × 3.1 × 12.40 = 29.95 = grams of urea in 24 hours.

324. For accurate determinations of the quantity of urea, one of the modifications of the Knop-Hüfner process is recommended (see " Manual," 4th ed., p. 343, and Charles' " Physiological Chem.," pp. 350 et seq.).

Uric Acid.

325. Acidulate 200 cc. of the filtered urine with 10 cc HCl, and set it aside in a cool place for forty-eight hours. Wash a small filter with dil. HCl, dry it, enclose it between two watch-glasses held together by a brass clamp, and determine the weight of the whole. Collect the crystals which have formed in the acidulated urine upon the weighed filter, detaching such crystals as adhere to the wall of the vessel by rubbing with a small section of rubber tubing slipped over the end of a glass rod, and washing the deposit on to the filter with portions of the filtrate. When the ppt. is all on the filter, wash it by the successive addition of small portions of H_2O until the filtrate is no longer acid. The filter and contents are now dried, enclosed between the watch-glasses, and weighed. This last weight, minus that first determined, is the weight of uric acid in 200 cc. urine; and this, multiplied by $\frac{1}{200}$ the amount of urine in twenty-four hours, is the amount in twenty-four hours.

The amount of wash-water used should not exceed 35 cc. If more should be used, add 0.043 mgm. to the weight of uric acid in 200 cc. urine for every extra cc. of wash-water.

Example. Urine in 24 hours = 1,230 cc.

Weight of watch-glasses, clamp, filter, and
uric acid   36.3275
Weight of watch-glasses, clamp, and filter   36.1948

Uric acid in 200 cc.   0.1327
Correction for wash-water   0.0004
45 cc. wash-water used . . . .043 × 10 = 0.43 mgm.

Uric acid in 200 cc. corrected   0.1331

$$\frac{0.1331 \times 1,230}{200} = 0.8185 = \text{grams uric acid in 24 hours.}$$

326. The normal elimination of uric acid in twenty-four hours is from 0.5 to 1.0 gm.

Albumin.

327. *Gravimetric method.*—Place 100 cc. of the clear urine in a beaker of 200 cc. capacity; if alkaline, acidulate faintly with acetic acid. Heat the beaker over the water-bath, add 1–2 gtt. acetic acid,

GLUCOSE.

largely diluted with water, when nearly boiling; continue boiling gently until the diffuse ppt. has collected in lumps. Have ready a small filter whose weight, with that of watch-glasses and clamp (see § 325), has been determined. Collect the coagulated albumin upon the filter, wash with H_2O containing a little HNO_3, then with boiling H_2O until the filtrate no longer forms a ppt. with $AgNO_3$, then with alcohol, and finally with ether. Dry the filter and contents in the air-oven, and weigh between the watch-glasses. The difference between this last weight and the one first determined is the weight of dry albumin in 100 cc. urine, which, multiplied by $\frac{1}{100}$ the quantity in twenty-four hours, gives the elimination of albumin in twenty-four hours.

If the urine be highly albuminous, it is best to operate upon 20 or 50 cc., diluted with 80 or 50 cc. H_2O, and multiply, to obtain the final result, by $\frac{1}{20}$ or $\frac{1}{50}$ the amount of urine in twenty-four hours.

Glucose.

328. *Fehling's method.*—The solution is made as follows:

I. Dissolve cupric sulfate   51.98 grams
    in water to   500.00 cc.

II. Dissolve Rochelle salt   259.9 grams
    in sodium hydroxid soln. sp. gr. 1.12 to 1,000 cc. (Piffard).

When required for use, one volume of I. is to be mixed with two volumes of II. The copper contained in 10 cc. of this mixture is precipitated completely, as cuprous oxid, by 0.05 gram of glucose.

329. To determine the quantity of sugar, place 10 cc. of the mixed soln. in a flask of about 250 cc. capacity, dilute with H_2O to about 30 cc., and heat to boiling. On the other hand, the urine to be tested is diluted, and thoroughly mixed with four volumes of H_2O if it be poor in sugar, or with nine volumes of H_2O if highly saccharine, and a burette filled with the mixture. When the Fehling soln. boils, add a few gtt. NH_4HO and then 5 cc. of the urine from the burette, boil again, and continue the alternate addition of diluted urine and boiling of the mixture until the blue color is quite faint. Now add the diluted urine in quantities of 1 cc. at a time, boiling after each addition until the blue color just disappears. Have ready a small filter, and, having filtered through it a few gtt. of the hot mixture, acidulate the filtrate with acetic acid, and add to it 1 gtt. soln. of potassium ferrocyanid. If a brownish tinge be produced, add another ½ cc. of dil. urine to the flask, boil, and test with ferrocyanid as before. Continue this proceeding until no brown tinge is produced. The burette reading, taken at this point, gives the number of cc. of dilute urine containing 0.05 gm. glucose, and this divided by 5 or 10, according as the urine was diluted with 4 or 9 volumes of H_2O, gives the number of cc. of urine containing 0.05 gm. sugar. The number of cc. urine passed in twenty-four hours divided by 20 times the number of cc. containing 0.05 gm. glucose, gives the elimination of glucose in twenty-four hours in grams.

Example. Urine in 24 hours = 2,436 cc.
Fehling's soln. used = 10 cc.
Urine diluted with 4 vols. H_2O.
Burette reading = 18.5 cc.

$\dfrac{18.5}{5} = 3.7 =$ cc. urine containing 0.05 gm. glucose.

$\dfrac{2,436}{3.7 \times 20} = 32.92 =$ grams glucose eliminated in 24 hours.

URINARY DEPOSITS.

330. Shake the urine to be examined, fill a conical glass (Fig. 17) with it, cover the glass with a watch-glass or glass plate, and set it aside until any solid particles have subsided to the bottom.

Crystalline deposits settle in a few hours, but if the urine have been found to contain albumin, and casts are consequently to be looked for, twelve hours must be allowed to elapse to insure complete deposition, unless a centrifugal be used.

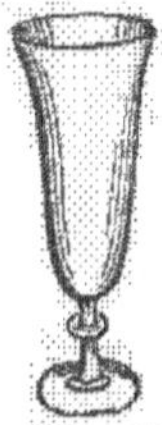

After the deposit has collected at the point of the glass, some of the sediment is removed with a pipette. Hold the pipette in such a manner that its upper opening is closed by the forefinger, and bring the point down into the layer of sediment, free the upper opening for an instant, close it again, and withdraw the pipette. Transfer a small quantity of urine and sediment from the pipette to a glass slide, upon which a ring of cement has been made and allowed to dry, put on a clean cover-glass, remove the excess of liquid from the slide with bibulous paper, and examine with the microscope.

FIG. 17.

Unorganized Deposits.

331. URIC ACID.—Deposits of uric acid occur in acid urines; are always crystalline, of the forms shown in Fig. 18, of which *b* are exceptional forms, and *a* of common occurrence; almost invariably of a color varying from light yellow to dark red or brown. Frequently they are of sufficient size to be visible to the unaided eye. Deposits of uric acid respond to the murexid test, § 266, and dissolve when warmed with NaHO soln.

332. AMORPHOUS, ACID URATES consist principally of acid sodium urate, accompanied sometimes with much smaller quantities of the potassium, calcium, and ammonium salts. The deposit is amorphous, composed of minute granular particles, sometimes colorless, but frequently yellow or red ("brick dust" or "lateritious" sediment), produced in acid urine.

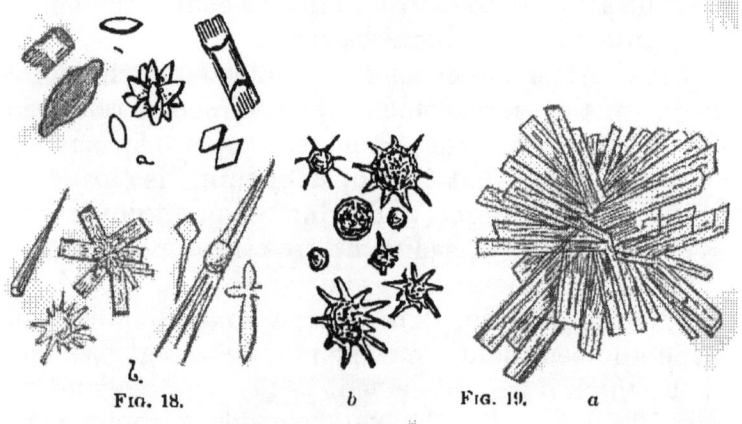

FIG. 18.   b   FIG. 19.   a

Urine cloudy from the presence of amorphous urates becomes clear when heated.

333. CRYSTALLINE URATES.—*Acid sodium urate* sometimes crystallizes from the urine undergoing acid or incipient alkaline fermentation, in the form of prisms arranged in stellate bundles (Fig. 19, *a*). Later in the fermentative process, when ammonia is produced, the highly colored spherical crystals, with or without spines (Fig. 19, *b*), of acid ammonium urate are produced.

334. CALCIUM OXALATE is observed sometimes in acid urine, accompanying crystals of uric acid, sometimes in alkaline or neutral urine along with crystals of triple phosphate. These crystals are usually very minute octahedra (Fig. 20, *a*), and occasionally in "dumb-bell" forms (Fig. 20, *b*).

335. AMMONIO-MAGNESIAN PHOSPHATE — *Triple phosphate*—occurs in slightly acid or alkaline urine, particularly of the shapes shown in Fig. 21, sufficiently large to be visible as shining specks when the vessel containing the urine is rotated in sunlight. Occasionally it forms star-shaped groups of feathery crystals.

336. CALCIUM PHOSPHATE is deposited under the

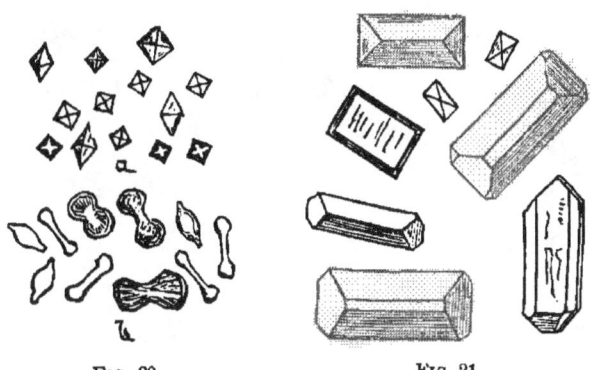

FIG. 20.   FIG. 21.

same conditions as ammonio-magnesian phosphate. The deposit is usually amorphous, and increases on the application of heat, but disappears on the addition of a mineral acid. Occasionally calcium phosphate crystallizes from the urine, either in wedge-shaped crystals, arranged in rosettes, their points uniting (Fig. 22), or in spherical crystals. or, more rarely, in dumb-bells.

337. LEUCIN AND TYROSIN always occur together, and are found only in urines containing biliary pigments. The former substance forms yellow, highly refracting spheres of varying size, marked with

URINARY DEPOSITS. 78

radiating and concentric striations (Fig. 23, *a*). Tyrosin crystallizes in bundles of delicate hair-like crystals, arranged in brush-like groups (Fig. 23, *b*).

338. CYSTIN is of rare occurrence. It appears as a yellowish deposit in pale, acid, or alkaline urine, which, when examined microscopically, is found to consist of hexagonal plates, either colorless or pig-

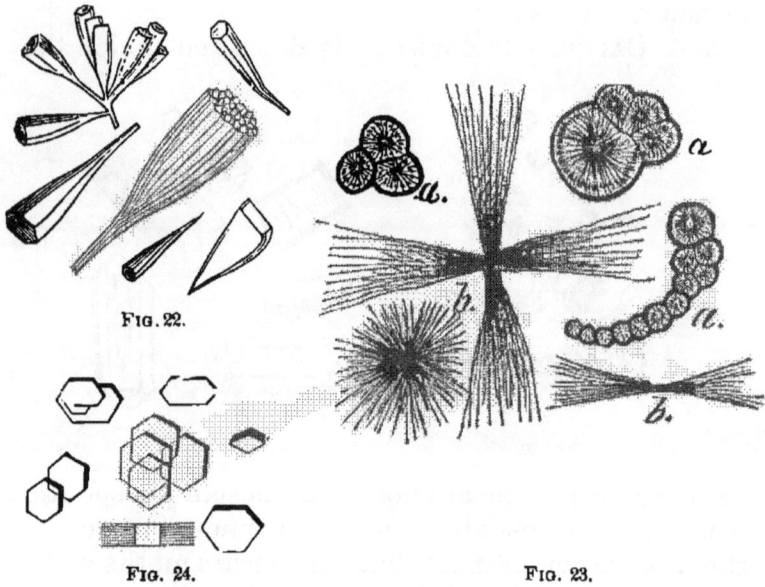

FIG. 22.   FIG. 24.   FIG. 23.

mented (Fig. 24). It dissolves in NH_4HO, and crystallizes out again on evaporation of the solution.

Organized Deposits.

339. MUCUS or PUS CORPUSCLES are rounded, granular cells, larger than blood-corpuscles, containing one or more nuclei (Fig. 25). Water causes them to swell up and lose their granular marking; the

URINARY DEPOSITS. 79

nuclei become more distinct, and the body of the cell gradually becomes invisible. Dilute acetic acid (20%) produces the same changes more rapidly.

340. EPITHELIUM.—The epithelial cells met with in urine are: 1. *Round epithelial cells*, from the convoluted tubes, the pelvis of the kidney, the bladder, and the male urethra; are rounded, granular bodies, larger than pus-corpuscles, containing a single nucleus (Fig. 26, *a*). 2. *Columnar or conical epithelial*

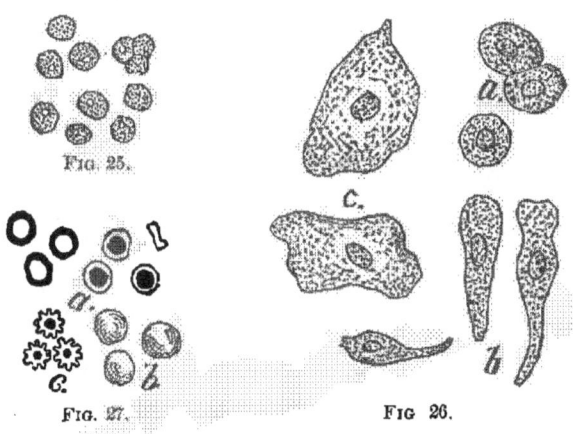

Fig. 25. Fig. 27. Fig. 26.

cells, from the pelvis of the kidney, the ureters and urethra, are elongated, conical bodies, granular, and containing a single nucleus near the middle (Fig. 26, *b*). 3. *Flat epithelial cells*, from the bladder and vagina, are large, irregular, scale-like bodies, faintly granular, and containing a single nucleus (Fig. 26, *c*).

341. BLOOD-CORPUSCLES appear in urine as rounded bodies, whose centres and peripheries alternate in light and shadow as the objective is moved toward or away from the slide (Fig. 27, *a*). If the urine be dilute, the blood-discs lose their concavity, swell up,

and no longer show alternations of light and shadow (Fig. 27, *b*); finally they become invisible. If the urine be concentrated, their concavity becomes greater, they shrink, and finally assume a crenated form (Fig. 27, *c*).

342. CASTS are moulds of the uriniferous tubules, of which the following varieties occur: 1. *Epithelial casts* are clear, cylindrical bodies, in whose surfaces epithelium from the tubules is embedded (Fig. 28, *a*).

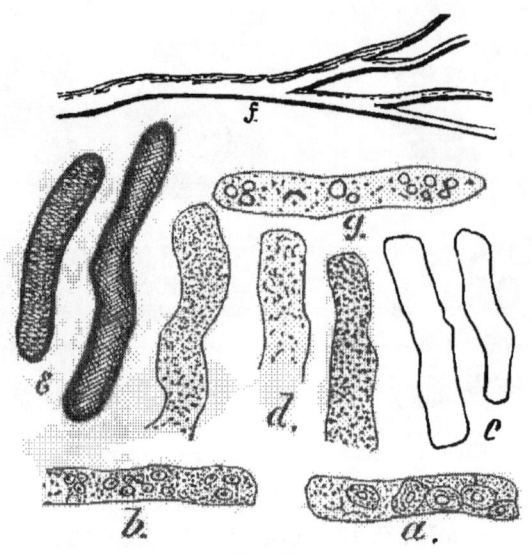

FIG. 28.

2. *Blood casts* are casts marked with granules and having blood-corpuscles embedded in them (Fig. 28, *b*). 3. *Hyaline casts* are perfectly clear, transparent cylinders, without any markings (Fig. 28, *c*), which being of about the same index of refraction as the urine, may be readily overlooked if the examination be not very carefully made. Their detection

is facilitated by adding a drop of a solution of eosin to the deposit before putting on the coverglass. 4. *Granular casts* are marked by granules resulting from the disintegration of epithelium and blood-corpuscles. They are either *highly granular* (Fig. 28, *d*), *moderately granular*, or *faintly granular*, as they contain more or less granular matter. 5. *Fatty casts*, or *oil casts*, contain oil globules (Fig. 28, *g*). 6. *Waxy casts* are somewhat similar to hya-

FIG. 29.

line casts in appearance, but more dense and somewhat resembling wax (Fig. 28, *e*). 7. *Mucous cases* are very long, frequently branching, transparent bodies (Fig. 28, *f*).

343. SPERMATOZOA are minute, tadpole-like bodies (Fig. 29), which, when present in urine, do not exhibit the vibrating motion with which they are endowed during life.

QUALITATIVE ANALYSIS OF URINARY CALCULI.

344. If the calculus be large, and if it is to be preserved, saw it in two with a hack-saw and use the sawdust for analysis, keeping that portion of the dust which is produced while sawing through the centre of the stone separate from the other. If the calculus be small, break it; separate the nucleus, if there be one, powder the nucleus and a portion of the body of the stone separately, and make an independent analysis of each.

345. In using the following scheme, take a separate portion of the powder for each operation, unless otherwise directed.

SCHEME OF ANALYSIS.

1. Heat on platinum foil until colorless:
    a. It is entirely volatile.................. 2
    b. A residue remains..................... 5
2. Moisten with HNO_3; evaporate to dryness over the water-bath; add NH_4HO:
    a. A red color is produced............... 3
    b. No red color is produced............. 4
3. Treat with KHO, without heating:
    a An ammoniacal odor is produced,
           Ammonium urate.
    b. No ammoniacal odor is produced,
           Uric acid.
4. a. The HNO_3 soln. becomes yellow when evaporated; the yellow residue becomes reddish-yellow on addition of KHO, and on heating with KHO, violet-red........................*Xanthin.*

URINARY CALCULI.

  b. The HNO_3 soln. becomes dark brown on evaporation.................... *Cystin.*
5. Moisten with HNO_3, evaporate to dryness over the water-bath; add NH_4HO:
  a. A red color is produced............. 6
  b. No red color is produced............. 9
6. Heat before the blowpipe on platinum foil:
  a. Fuses.......................... 7
  b. Does not fuse.................... 8
7. Bring into blue flame on clean platinum wire:
  a. Flame colored yellow...... *Sodium urate.*
  b. Flame violet when observed through blue glass................ *Potassium urate.*
8. The residue from 6:
  a. Dissolves in dil. HCl with effervescence; the soln. forms a white ppt. with ammonium oxalate.......... *Calcium urate.*
  b. Dissolves with slight effervescence in dil. H_2SO_4; the soln. neutralized with NH_4-HO gives a white ppt. with Na_2HPO_4.
  Magnesium urate.
9. Heat on platinum foil:
  a. It fuses. *Ammonio-magnesian phosphate.*
  b. It does not fuse................10
10. The residue from 9, moistened with H_2O, and tested with red litmus paper, is:
  a. Alkaline 11
  b. Not alkaline......... *Tricalcic phosphate.*
11. The original substance dissolves in HCl:
  a. With effervescence.. *Calcium carbonate.*
  b. Without effervescence.. *Calcium oxalate*

DETECTION OF POISONS.

346. The identification of any of the accessible poisons when unmixed with other substances does not present any serious difficulty. When, however, the poison is mixed with a large proportion of foreign substances, as in an article of food, in the contents of the stomach or in the viscera, the reactions upon which we depend are masked or modified to such a degree that no reliance is to be placed upon them. Consequently, in searching for a poison in organic mixtures the first step, preliminary to the actual testing, is the separation of the poison from other substances in a condition as pure as possible and with as little loss as may be.

347. Analytically, poisons are divided into three classes, according to the methods used in their separation from organic mixtures: 1. Volatile Poisons. 2. Mineral Poisons. 3. Organic Poisons.

VOLATILE POISONS.

348. Those poisons which may be separated from the materials under examination by the process of distillation are included in this class. The most important are: Phosphorus, Hydrocyanic Acid, Alcohol, Ether, Chloroform, Chloral, Benzene and its derivatives, including Carbolic Acid.

349. To separate poisons of this class, the contents of the stomach (or other substance to be examined), diluted with H_2O if necessary, are slightly acidulated with dilute H_2SO_4 and placed in a flask, which should be only half filled; the flask is then connected with a Liebig's condenser and heated over a sand-bath. The distillation is continued until two-thirds of the liquid have distilled over, and the distillate is collected in three separate portions. The distillates are then to be tested for individual poisons by suitable reagents.

Phosphorus. P.

350. The material gives off an odor of garlic, and (in absence of alcohol, ether, oil of turpentine, and other substances) is luminous when shaken in the dark.

351. It is advisable in cases of suspected phosphorus poisoning to spread the suspected material out on a clean plate, and examine it *in a dark room* for any luminous points. It must not be forgotten, however, that muscular and other animal tissues may be phosphorescent in absence of phosphorus.

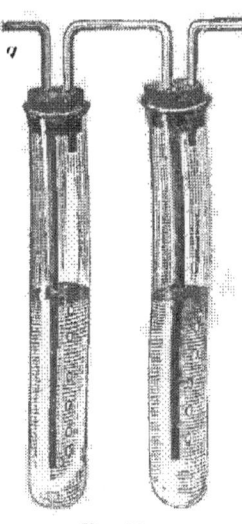

Fig. 30.

352. If the presence of phosphorus be suspected, the process, § 349, is to be somewhat modified. It is to be conducted in a dark room with a screen interposed between the condenser and the source of heat. If no luminous ring (§ 353) be observed when one-third of the liquid has distilled over, remove the condenser and substitute for it the apparatus shown in Fig. 30, charged with $AgNO_3$ soln., and continue the distillation while a current of CO_2 is passed through the entire apparatus. If phosphorus be present, the $AgNO_3$ soln.

PHOSPHORUS.

blackens. If this occur, collect the black deposit formed and introduce it through the funnel F into the apparatus (Fig. 31) in which hydrogen is generated, and ignite the escaping gas at a platinum jet, C. In the presence of phosphorus, a bright green core appears in the flame.

353. During the distillation, § 352, a luminous band is observed at the point of greatest condensation in the condenser. If, however, the liquid in the

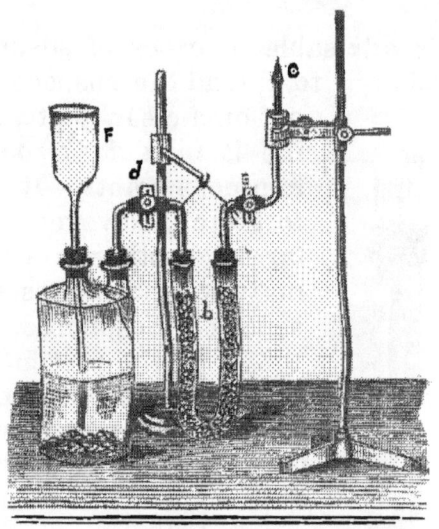

FIG. 31.

flask contain alcohol or ether, this luminous band does not appear until after one-third of the liquid has been distilled. If oil of turpentine be present, the luminous band does not appear at all.

354. Examine the distillate for globules of P, which are recognized by their yellow, waxy appearance, their odor, their luminosity in the dark, and the bluing of paper moistened with potassium iodid and starch, when exposed to the vapors which they give off.

355. ANTIDOTES.—No chemical antidote known. Remove unabsorbed poison with stomach-pump, $CuSO_4$, or apomorphin. Old French oil of turpentine. Prohibit fats and oils, which favor absorption.

Hydrocyanic Acid—Prussic Acid. HCN.

For the analytical characters of hydrocyanic acid, see cyanids, §§ 45 to 51.

356. ANTIDOTES.—A mixture of ferrous and ferric sulfates dissolved in H_2O and alkalized with KHO is a chemical antidote. The action of the poison is usually so rapid, however, that it is of little service. Stomach-pump, cold affusion, artificial respiration, galvanism, inhalation of ammonia, of chlorin (?). Atropin hypodermically (?).

Alcohol. C_2H_6HO.

357. Heat with a small quantity of a cooled mixture of H_2SO_4 and aqueous soln. of potassium dichromate: the liquid turns green, and the peculiar odor of aldehyde is given off.

358. Dissolve in the liquid a small quantity of iodin, add KHO soln. guttatim until the liquid is just decolorized, and warm: a yellowish, crystalline ppt. immediately or after a time, and the odor of iodoform.

359. Add HNO_3 and warm: odor of nitrous ether. Add soln. mercurous nitrate with excess HNO_3, and heat: a yellow-gray ppt. Collect ppt., wash, and dry: explodes when struck with hammer.

360. Mix slowly with an equal volume H_2SO_4, add some powdered sodium acetate, and heat: odor of acetic ether.

Chloroform. $CHCl_3$.

361. Add a few gtt. anilin to 3 cc. alcoholic soln. of KHO, and then 2 cc. of the liquid to be tested, and heat. In the presence of chloroform an intense, disagreeable, and characteristic odor, due to the formation of isobenzonitril, is produced.

362. Dissolve about 0.01 gm. of β naphthol in a small quantity of KHO soln., warm, and add the suspected liquid: a blue color is produced.

363. Dissolve in 1 cc. of the liquid under examination 0.05 gm. resorcin, add 5 gtt. liq. sodæ, and heat to boiling: a red color. The same effect is produced with chloral.

364. Place the liquid to be examined, which should be faintly acidulated with H_2SO_4 if not already acid, in a flask. Fit the flask with a cork, through which pass two right-angled tubes, one of which dips to near the bottom of the flask. Connect this longer tube with a bellows or gasometer, from which a slow current of air is made to pass through the apparatus during the process. The shorter tube is connected with about a foot of Bohemian tubing, whose other end communicates with a right-angled tube dipping into a solution of $AgNO_3$, or with a bulb apparatus filled with $AgNO_3$ soln. Heat the flask over a waterbath, and heat about six inches of the Bohemian tube to bright redness. In the presence of $CHCl_3$ a white ppt. of AgCl, soluble in NH_4HO, insoluble in HNO_3, is formed in the $AgNO_3$ soln.

365. ANTIDOTES.—No chemical antidote is known. Cold douche, galvanism, fresh air, artificial respiration, inhalation of ammonia.

Chloral—Trichloraldehyde. C_2HCl_3O.

366. The substance to be examined is first treated

as in § 364. If no ppt. be produced in the $AgNO_3$ soln., the liquid in the flask is rendered *alkaline* with KHO soln., and the process continued. If now a ppt. be formed in the $AgNO_3$ soln., the flask is connected with a condenser and more strongly heated. Portions of the distillate are then tested according to §§ 361, 362 for chloroform, resulting from the decomposition of the chloral by the alkali.

367. ANTIDOTES.—No chemical antidote. Stomach-pump, tea, coffee, galvanism, artificial respiration, cold douche, ammonia by inhalation.

Phenol—Carbolic Acid. C_6H_5HO.

368. Odor of carbolic acid.

369. Mix with one-quarter volume NH_4HO; add 1-2 gtt. sodium hypochlorite soln., and warm: a blue or green color. Add HCl to acid reaction: turns red.

370. Add 1-2 gtt. of the liquid to a little HCl, mix; add 1 gtt. HNO_3 : a purple-red color.

371. Boil with HNO_3 as long as red fumes are given off; neutralize with KHO: a yellow, crystalline ppt.

372. Add a few gtt. $FeSO_4$ soln : a lilac color.

373. Float liquid to be tested on H_2SO_4; add a very small quantity of powdered KNO_3 : violet color.

374. Add excess of bromin water: a yellowish-white ppt.

375. ANTIDOTES.—Emetics, white of egg, stimulants.

MINERAL POISONS.

MINERAL ACIDS AND ALKALIES.

376. These substances are corrosives rather than true poisons, as their deleterious effects are produced by destruction of or injury to important viscera with which they come into immediate contact, while the true poisons act only after absorption into the circulation.

377. The presence of strong acids or alkalies in the stomach is indicated by corrosion or even perforation of the viscus, and by a strongly acid or alkaline reaction of the contents. It must not be forgotten that the contents of the stomach may have been rendered alkaline after the ingestion of acids, or acid after alkalies have been taken, by the administration of antidotes.

378. In all cases of corrosion by mineral acids or alkalies (except nitric acid) a quantitative analysis should be made, and the amount found compared with that normally present, as sulfates, chlorids, and salts of sodium and potassium are normal constituents of the body.

N. B.—The color tests for free mineral acids (methyl-violet, Congo red, phloroglucin-vanillin, etc.) fail in the presence of peptones and other organic substances, and are therefore useless as applied to contents of the stomach.

For the analytical characters of **Sulfuric Acid**, H_2SO_4, see §§ 71 to 76; **Nitric Acid**, HNO_3, see §§ 54 to 57; and **Hydrochloric Acid, HCl**, see §§ 33 to 36.

379. ANTIDOTES FOR MINERAL ACIDS.—Magnesia usta, suspended in water, or, failing this, soap.

Neither the alkaline carbonates, chalk, or magnesium carbonate should be used, as the gas liberated from them may cause serious distension of the weakened walls of the stomach. The stomach-pump should be used only if the case be seen very early, and then with great care. It will frequently be necessary to sustain life by nutritive enemata. Opium to allay pain.

380. For the analytical characters of **Caustic Potassa—Potassium Hydroxid, KHO**, see §§ 179 to 184; **Caustic Soda—Sodium Hydroxid, NaHO**, see §§ 175 to 178; and **Aqua Ammoniæ—Ammonium Hydroxid, NH_4HO**, see §§ 185 to 188.

In cases of fatal corrosion by KHO, or of poisoning by the K salts, a quantitative determination is necessary.

381. ANTIDOTES TO THE ALKALIES.—Dilute vinegar or lemon juice, milk. Opium to allay pain. Nutritive enemata if necessary.

METALLIC POISONS.

382. Preliminary to the separation of mineral poisons from the tissues or contents of the stomach, the organic matter must be destroyed by oxidation, as completely as is possible, without risk of loss of the substances sought for. This is best effected by the method of Fresenius and Von Babo. The substances under examination, hashed if solid, are diluted with water. About 50 cc. HCl* and a small quantity of powdered potassium chlorate are added,

* Hydrochloric acid cannot be bought sufficiently pure for this purpose. It must be made in the laboratory from pure NaCl and arsenic-free H_2SO_4.

and the whole heated over the water-bath. Small portions of $KClO_3$, and more HCl *if necessary*, are added from time to time, until the mass is reduced to a yellow liquid on whose surface floats a layer of oil. The decomposition is accelerated by stirring and crushing any solid particles with the flattened end of a glass rod. When decomposition is complete, the liquid is allowed to cool, and filtered. If the filtrate smell of Cl, it is heated over the water-bath and treated with CO_2 until free of Cl. The liquid is now treated with H_2S for periods of an hour at a time, at intervals of twelve hours during two or three days; the flask containing it being kept corked during the intervals. A ppt. is always formed if a portion of the body has been operated on. This ppt. is collected on a filter and the filtrate (C) preserved. The ppt. is slightly washed and treated on the filter with yellow NH_4HS, concentrated at first, afterward dilute, so long as anything is dissolved. Any solid matter remaining undissolved on the filter is subsequently examined (B). The filtrate is evaporated to dryness in a porcelain capsule. To the residue 25 cc. H_2O, 2 cc. HCl, and a little $KClO_3$ are added, and the whole heated over the water-bath. The liquid is stirred until hot, small quantities of $KClO_3$ are added from time to time, and the mixture stirred until all is dissolved except a little sulfur. The liquid is then treated with CO_2 over the water-bath till free of Cl, filtered, cooled, and treated with H_2S as before. The ppt. is collected on a filter and washed with H_2O containing a little H_2S, until the washings after boiling with HNO_3 fail to give *any* cloudiness with $AgNO_3$. The ppt. is now dissolved off the filter with NH_4HS, he solution evaporated in a porcelain capsule, the residue moistened with fuming HNO_3, dried over the water-bath, moistened with H_2O and dried two or three times, and finally fused with a mixture of $NaNO_3$ and Na_2CO_3 until it is colorless or only contains a black powder. After cooling, the fused mass is dissolved in H_2O, treated with CO_2, and the solution filtered; the ppt., if any, on the filter (A) is examined as below. The filtrate is treated with excess of H_2SO_4 and heated, first over the water-bath, and afterward at a higher temperature, until copious white fumes are given off; after cooling, the residue is examined for ARSENIC.

The ppt. A contains any Sb, Sn, or Cu (part) that may have been present. It is first, if black, treated with hot dil. HNO_3. The soln. so obtained is examined for COPPER. If the soln. from which it was filtered was turbid from the presence of a white material, the filter with adherent matter, insoluble in dil. HNO_3, after having been washed, is dried and burnt in a porcelain crucible, a small quantity of KCN is added to the ash, and the mixture fused for about ten minutes. After cooling, the contents of the crucible are treated with H_2O, and washed with H_2O by decantation, so long as anything is dissolved. The remaining metallic particles are treated with dil. HCl, the liquid separated, after warming on the water-bath, and tested for TIN. If any undissolved metallic particles remain, they are dissolved in hot concentrated HCl, and the soln. is tested for ANTIMONY.

If the portion B, insoluble in NH_4HS, be white, it contains no poisonous metal. If it be colored, it is heated with HNO_3 so long as red fumes are given off, more HNO_3 being added if necessary, evaporated nearly to dryness, a little dil. H_2SO_4 added, allowed to stand for a time, and filtered. The filtrate is tested for BISMUTH and COPPER. The residue, if any, is treated with tartaric acid and then with excess of NH_4HO, boiled, and filtered. The filtrate is tested for LEAD. The residue, if any, is dissolved in aqua regia, the soln. evaporated, the residue dissolved in H_2O, acidulated with HCl, and tested for MERCURY.

The liquid C contains any BARIUM, CHROMIUM, or ZINC that may have been present in the substances examined.

Arsenic. As.

383. Heat a small quantity As_2O_3 in a reduction tube.* Minute octahedral crystals of As_2O_3, which present brilliant reflections when the tube is rotated in sunlight, are deposited above the heated portion of the tube (Fig. 32, p. 96).

384. Heat a small quantity of Paris green in a reduction tube: crystals of As_2O_3 are formed, as in § 383.

385. Heat a small portion of elementary As in a long reduction tube: a brilliant steel-gray, brown, or black metallic-looking band is formed.

386. Cut off the bottom of the tube used in § 385; heat the band, holding the tube in an inclined position: the metallic band disappears, and above the point which it occupied a crystalline sublimate of As_2O_3 is deposited.

387. Put a small quantity of As_2O_3 into a long reduction tube, and above it a splinter of charcoal. Heat the charcoal first, then the As_2O_3: a metallic

* A glass tube, 3-4 mm. in internal diameter and 8 cent. long, closed at one end.

band. as in § 385, is formed. Cut off the bottom of the tube and heat as in § 386: crystals of As_2O_3 are formed.

388. Acidulate soln. H_3AsO_3 with 2 gtt. HCl, and pass H_2S through the soln.: a yellow ppt. of As_2S_3 is formed. Warm the contents of the tube, agitate, collect the ppt. on a filter, and wash. Divide the ppt. into four parts on four watch-glasses.

389. Add NH_4HS to one watch-glass: the ppt. dissolves.

390. Another portion of ppt. § 388 is treated with NH_4HO: it dissolves.

391. Another portion of ppt. § 388 is treated with HCl: it does not dissolve.

392. Mix the remaining portion, after drying, with potassium ferrocyanid, and heat a portion in a long reduction tube: a metallic band is formed. Cut off end of tube; heat as in § 386; crystals of As_2O_3.

393. To soln H_3AsO_4 in a test-tube add KHO to alkaline reaction, and treat with H_2S: no ppt. is formed. Add HCl: a yellow ppt. is formed as in § 388.

394. Acidulate soln. H_3AsO_4 with HCl, and treat with H_2S: the liquid first turns yellow and cloudy, but the yellow ppt. of As_2S_3 only begins to form after a time.

395. Put 5 cc. H_2O into a porcelain capsule, add 1 gtt NH_4HO, and then $CuSO_4$ until the ppt. formed no longer redissolves. To the liquid so obtained add about 1 cc. of the liquid under examination: a green ppt. Stir the mixture and transfer it in about equal portions to two test-tubes. To one tube add HNO_3: the ppt. dissolves, and the liquid becomes colorless. To the other test-tube add NH_4HO: the ppt. dissolves, forming a blue soln.

ARSENIC. 96

396. Put 5 cc. H_2O into a porcelain capsule; add 1 gtt. NH_4HO, and then $AgNO_3$ soln. until a permanent ppt. remains. Add 1 cc. H_3AsO_3 soln.: a canary-yellow ppt. If the ppt. do not appear, test the reaction of the contents of the capsule, and render neutral by the *cautious* addition of very dil. HNO_3 or NH_4HO. Transfer to two test-tubes, and add HNO_3 to one. NH_4HO to the other: both clear to colorless solutions.

397. Repeat the test as in § 396, using a soln. of H_3AsO_4 in place of H_3AsO_3: a brick-red ppt., which also dissolves in HNO_3 and in NH_4HO.

398. *Reinsch's test.*—To 5 cc. H_2O in a test-tube add 0.5 cc. HCl and a slip of sheet Cu 2 mm. wide and 2 cent. long; boil about five minutes, adding H_2O to supply loss by evaporation. If the Cu remain *perfectly* bright, the materials are pure; if the Cu become *even faintly* dimmed, the materials (Cu or HCl) are impure, and others must be substituted.

Having proven the purity of the reagents, put about 5 cc. of the liquid under examination into a test-tube, add 0.5 cc. HCl and a slip of Cu, and boil. The Cu becomes gray, then black. Remove the Cu, wash it in H_2O, dry between filter paper, taking care not to detach the black deposit. Place the Cu strip in and about 3 cent. from one end of a glass tube about 3 mm. in internal diameter and 15 cent. long. Warm the tube cautiously, holding it at an angle of 45° to the horizontal, until all moisture is driven off, then

FIG. 32.

ARSENIC. 97

hold the tube at the same angle in the flame, so that the Cu is heated to bright redness. A white band is formed above the point at which the Cu was heated. Rotate the tube in the sunlight; brilliant, diamond-like reflections are seen. Examine the white band with a magnifier; it is found to consist of octahedral crystals of As_2O_3 (Fig. 32) (see §§ 406, 409, 412).

399. *Marsh's test.*—Place some granulated zinc

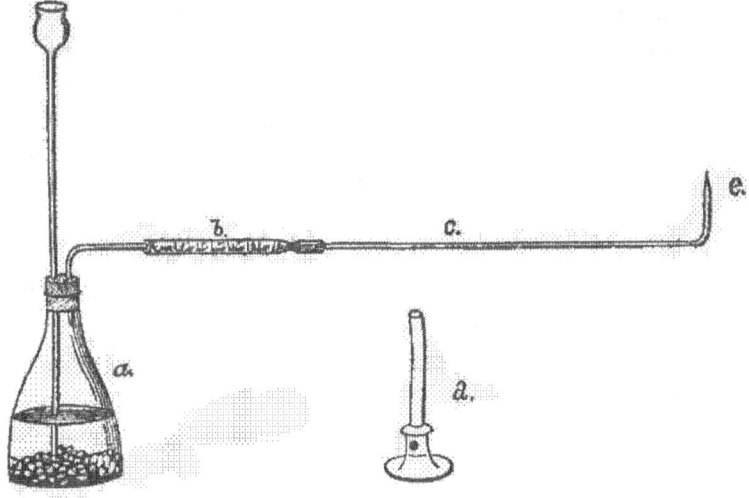

FIG. 33.

in a flask of 100 cc. capacity; fit the cork carrying a funnel tube and right-angled tube (*a*, Fig. 33). Connect the right-angled tube with the drying tube *b*, filled with fragments of $CaCl_2$ or CaO between loose plugs of cotton, and connect this in turn with the Bohemian tube *c*. Pour dil. H_2SO_4 through the funnel tube in small quantities at a time, so that a moderate evolution of H_2 results. After twenty

ARSENIC.   98

minutes, light the burner *d*, and the gas escaping at *e*, and, after another half-hour, examine the tube at *c*. If the tube be *perfectly clean*, the Zn and H_2SO_4 are free from arsenic; but if any deposit have formed at *c*, the reagents contain As and must be discarded. Having thus proved the purity of the chemicals, introduce the liquid to be tested, strongly acidulated with H_2SO_4, through the funnel tube in small portions at a time, and at such a rate that two hours would be consumed in adding 25 cc. If As be present a black or brown, single or double, metallic "mirror" is produced at *c*. After the mirror has become quite distinct, the tube *c* may be disconnected from *b*, another tube fitted, and a second mirror collected. Now extinguish the burner, and hold a short section (about 2 cent.), cut from the bottom of a test-tube, over the flame at *e*, and, after a few moments, remove and examine it. If As be present in sufficient quantity, the brilliant octahedral crystals of As_2O_3 will be found deposited on the glass. Next hold the cover of a porcelain crucible *in* the flame at *e* for a short time: a brown stain is formed on the porcelain. Collect several similar stains on porcelain, and examine them as follows: 1. Moisten one with sodium hypochlorite soln.: it dissolves instantly. 2. Moisten with NH_4HS soln., and warm: it dissolves slowly. 3. Evaporate the soln. 2 to dryness: a yellow residue remains. 4 Obtain three residues as in 3. Moisten one with NH_4HO, the other with HCl: the former dissolves, the latter does not   5. Moisten the third residue 4 with HNO_3: it dissolves. Evaporate to dryness: a white residue remains. Moisten with $AgNO_3$ soln.: it turns brick-red.

Lastly, take one of the tubes c in which a mirror has been formed, cut off the bent portion, and, holding the tube at an angle of 45° to the horizontal, cautiously heat the mirror: it disappears, and above it a white ring is deposited, consisting of the brilliant octahedral crystals of As_2O_3.

Marsh's test is the most delicate and reliable of the tests for arsenic. Great caution is, however, required that the chemicals used do not themselves contain arsenic.

400. Antidotes.—Emetics, stomach-pump, dialyzed iron, ferric hydroxid. The last-named is made by adding excess of aqua ammoniæ to liq. ferri tersulfatis, collecting the ppt. in a piece of muslin, and washing at the tap until the washings do not smell of ammonia. It is to be given moist, and in quantities at least twenty times as great as the amount of As_2O_3 to be neutralized.

Antimony. Sb.

401. To 5 cc. of the soln. to be tested add 2 gtt. HCl: a white ppt. of Sb_2O_3, if the soln. be not too dilute. Continue the addition of HCl: the ppt. redissolves.

402. Treat the soln. from § 401 with H_2S: an orange-red ppt. Collect the ppt. on a filter; wash with H_2O and place portions in three test-tubes.

403. Add NH_4HS to a portion of the ppt. from § 402: it dissolves.

404. Add NH_4HO to a portion of the ppt. from § 402: it does not dissolve.

405. Add HCl to a portion of the ppt. from § 402, and warm: it dissolves.

406. Apply *Reinsch's test* as directed in § 398: a stain, like that produced by arsenic, is formed upon the Cu. Upon heating the Cu in the glass tube, a white band is produced as in the case of As, but this band *consists of amorphous material* (Sb_2O_3), *not of crystals*.

407. Apply *Marsh's test* as directed in § 399. A metallic mirror, closely resembling that consisting of As, is formed in the tube *c*, Fig. 33; it differs, however, from the arsenical mirror in being situated nearer to the heated portion of the tube, in disappearing less rapidly when heated in the tube through which a current of air is passing, and in yielding an *amorphous* in place of a crystalline sublimate when so heated. The stains produced on porcelain differ from those consisting of As, in that: 1. They are insoluble in sodium hypochlorite soln. 2. They dissolve quickly in NH_4HS. 3. The residue of evaporation of the soln. from 2 is orange-red in color, is soluble in warm HCl, and insoluble in NH_4HO. 4. The residue of evaporation of the soln. from 2, when dissolved in warm HNO_3 and evaporated, leaves a white residue which does not become colored on addition of $AgNO_3$.

N. B.—If the method described in § 382 have been followed, As and Sb will have been separated, the latter having been precipitated from the soln. before the liquid is introduced into the Marsh apparatus, and, consequently, the two elements cannot be mistaken for one another.

408. ANTIDOTES.—Warm water to produce emesis if it have not occurred, stomach-pump, tannin (decoction of oak bark, cinchona, nutgalls, tea).

Bismuth. Bi.

For analytical characters of bismuth, see §§ 155 to 162.

409. When *Reinsch's test* is applied to a soln. containing Bi, the Cu becomes stained as with As and Sb, but no sublimate is formed when it is heated in the glass tube.

Copper. Cu. See §§ 220 to 226.

410. ANTIDOTES.—Stomach-pump, albumen.

Lead. Pb. See §§ 148 to 154.

411. ANTIDOTES.—Magnesium or sodium sulfate; stomach pump; emetics.

Mercury. Hg. See §§ 227 to 235.

412. Apply *Reinsch's test* to a soln. of $HgCl_2$: the Cu is stained as with As, Sb, and Bi, but when heated in the glass tube it yields a sublimate consisting of minute globules of Hg.

413. Immerse a bar of Zn, around which a strip of dentist's gold foil has been wound so as to leave exposed alternate surfaces of Zn and Au, in dil. soln. $HgCl_2$, acidulated with HCl. The Au is covered with a silvery film, and, when heated in a glass tube, yields a sublimate consisting of globules of Hg.

414. ANTIDOTES.—White of egg, followed in a few moments by an emetic, or stomach-pump.

Barium. Ba. See §§ 202 to 205.

415. ANTIDOTES.—Magnesium or sodium sulfate.

Zinc. Zn. See §§ 213 to 219.

416. ANTIDOTES.—Milk, white of egg, tea, tannin.

VEGETABLE POISONS.

417. In this class are included the alkaloids, glucosids, and vegetable acids. Their separation from organic mixtures, contents of stomach, organs, etc., is best effected by a combination of the Stas-Otto and Dragendorff methods. The substances to be examined, hashed if solid, are placed in a flask and covered with twice their weight of alcohol;* alcoholic solution of tartaric acid is then added, during agitation, until the contents of the flask are distinctly acid. The mouth of the flask is closed with a cork, through which passes a glass tube of 8 mm. internal diameter and about a metre long. open at both ends, and the flask warmed over the water bath about two hours. The contents of the flask are allowed to cool, filtered through a filter moistened with alcohol, and the insol. portion washed with alcohol. The alcoholic filtrate and washings are evaporated in a porcelain capsule at a temperature of 35° C. (95° Fahr.) until the alcohol is removed. The aqueous liquid remaining is cooled, filtered, and the filtrate evaporated to the consistence of syrup. To the syrupy residue a few gtt. absolute alcohol are added and the mixture thoroughly stirred. The addition of absolute alcohol in small portions, during constant stirring, is continued so long as any precipitate is formed. The alcoholic liquid is filtered off and the residue washed with alcohol. The filtrate and washings are evaporated to the consistence of syrup, and the residue dissolved

*Alcohol for this purpose must be purified by dissolving in it tartaric acid to strongly acid reaction, and distilling over the water-bath.

in H_4O. The distinctly acid aqueous soln. is transferred to a bulb funnel (Fig. 34), in which it is agitated with different solvents as follows:

The acid, aqueous liquid is agitated with petroleum ether, the ethereal layer separated and evaporated. This treatment, like all of the subsequent agitations, is repeated so long as the solvent dissolves anything. The petroleum ether leaves a residue, Residue I., which contains principally fatty, resinous, and pigmentary substances.

The acid, aqueous liquid is next agitated with benzene, which is evaporated in several watch-glasses This, Residue II., may contain colchicin, digitalin, and small quantities of veratrin and physostigmin.

The acid, aqueous liquid is then agitated with chloroform, which is evaporated in watch-glasses, yielding Residue III , which may contain picrotoxin and digitaleïn and traces of brucin, narcotin, physostigmin, and veratrin.

The acid, aqueous liquid is again agitated with petroleum ether to remove $CHCl_3$, the ether separated, and the aqueous liquid rendered alkaline with NH_4HO.

The alkaline, aqueous liquid is agitated with petroleum ether, which, on separation and evaporation in watch glasses, leaves Residue IV., which may contain coniïn and nicotin, and traces of brucin, strychnin, and veratrin.

The alkaline, aqueous liquid is next agitated with benzene, which is evaporated, yielding Residue V., in which atropin, hyoscyamin, narcotin, strychnin, aconitin. brucin, physostigmin, and veratrin may be found.

The alkaline, aqueous liquid is then agitated with chloroform, which, on evaporation, leaves Residue VI., which may contain the opium alkaloids in small quantity.

The alkaline, aqueous liquid is lastly agitated with amylic alcohol, from which Residue VII., in which morphin will be found if present in the substances examined, is obtained by evaporation.

Finally, curarin, if present, will remain in the aqueous liquid, which may also contain oxalic acid.

General Reactions of Alkaloids.

418. Add to an acidulated soln. of an alkaloid a soln. of potassium iodhydrargyrate (made by dissolving 13.546 gm. $HgCl_2$ and 49.8 gm. KI in 1 L. H_2O): a white or yellow ppt.

N. B.—This reaction, like the subsequent ones, is best performed by placing a drop of the liquid under examination and one of the reagent near each other on a slip of black glass and bringing the two together with a pointed glass rod.

419 Add to an acidulated soln. of an alkaloid a soln. of phosphomolybdic acid; a white or yellow ppt.

420. Add to an acidulated soln. of an alkaloid a soln. of phosphotungstic acid; a white, flocculent ppt.

421. The following reagents also produce ppts in faintly acidulated solns. of alkaloids: iodin in potassium iodid, brown; tannin, white or yellow; platinic chlorid, yellowish, usually becoming crystalline; auric chlorid, yellowish; phosphoantimonic acid, white; potassium iodid and cadmium iodid, white or yellow; picric acid, yellow.

Morphin.

422. Moisten a crystal with HNO_3: an orange color, changing to yellow.

423. Moisten with H_2SO_4: the alkaloid dissolves, forming a colorless soln. Warm until white fumes are given off, cool, introduce a trace of HNO_3: a red-violet color.

424. Dissolve a crystal of iodic acid in H_2O, and shake a part of the soln. with $CHCl_3$: the latter should not be colored. Add to a soln. of a morphin salt a few gtt. of the iodic acid soln., and agitate: the liquid assumes a yellow color. Add a gtt. of $CHCl_3$, and agitate: the $CHCl_3$ which separates at the bottom is colored violet. Float some dil. NH_4HO on the surface of the liquid: the test-tube will contain different colored layers; violet below, then yellow, dark yellow or brown, and faintly yellowish.

425. Moisten a crystal of morphin with, or add to a neutral soln. of one of its salts, a soln. of neutral Fe_2Cl_6: a blue color.

426. To a crystal of morphin add a soln. of molybdic acid in H_2SO_4 (Fröhde's reagent): a violet color, changing to blue, dirty green, and faint pink. Water discharges the color.

427. Add NH_4HO to $AgNO_3$ soln. until the ppt. is nearly dissolved, filter, add soln. of a morphin salt, and warm: a gray ppt. Filter off the liquid and add to it HNO_3: a red or pink color.

428. Heat morphin with conc. H_2SO_4 to 200° C. (392° F.) until green-black; add a drop of the liquid cautiously to H_2O: the solution turns blue. Shake a portion with ether: the ether turns purple. Shake a portion with chloroform: the chloroform turns blue.

429. Warm the solid alkaloid with conc. H_2SO_4; add cautiously a few drops of a 30% alcoholic soln. of KHO: a yellow color is produced, changing to dirty red, then steel blue and sky-blue, and. with a further quantity of KHO soln., cherry-red.

430. Add soln. Fe_2Cl_6 (2-16) to soln. potassium ferricyanid (1-50): the mixture remains yellow (a blue color is due to impurity of reagents). Add morphin soln.: a deep blue color.

431. ANTIDOTES.—Stomach-pump; wash out stomach with H_2O holding powdered charcoal in suspension, or with infusion of tea. $ZnSO_4$. Keep patient awake. Atropin?

Meconic Acid.

432. To portions of the acid in three watch-glasses add Fe_2Cl_6 soln.: a red color is produced. To one watch-glass add dil. HCl: the color is not discharged. To the second watch-glass add $HgCl_2$ soln.: the color is not discharged. To the third watch-glass add sodium hypochlorite soln.: the color is discharged.

433. Add Fe_2Cl_6 soln. to a thiocyanate in a watch-glass: a red color, similar to that with meconic acid, is produced Add $HgCl_2$ soln : the color is discharged.

Strychnin.

434. Place a minute drop of a soln. of a strychnin salt on the tongue: a persistent, intensely bitter taste.

435. Add H_2SO_4: the alkaloid (or its salts) dissolves, forming a colorless soln. Draw through the soln. a fragment of a crystal of potassium dichromate; it is followed by a streak of color; at first blue (very transitory and frequently not observed), then a brilliant violet which slowly changes to rose pink and finally to yellow.

436. Evaporate a drop of soln. of a strychnin salt on a slip of Pt foil, moisten the residue with concentrated H_2SO_4, connect the foil with the + pole of a Grove cell, and bring a Pt wire, connected with the — pole, in contact with the surface of the acid: a violet color on the surface of the foil.

437. Moisten a fragment of strychnin with a soln. of iodic acid in H_2SO_4: a yellow color, changing to brick-red and then to violet-red.

438. Let an assistant hold a small frog by the hind legs. Raise the skin of the back at the root of the legs with a forceps, make a small incision with a scissors, and allow a few gtt. of a very dilute soln. of a salt of strychnin to flow into the lymph pouch. Place the frog under a glass shade: within ten minutes the animal has violent tetanic spasms, with opisthotonos or emprosthotonos, increasing in frequency, and provoked on the slightest touch, or by blowing upon the surface.

439. Add a few gtt. of a dil. soln. of potassium dichromate to a soln. of a strychnin salt: a yellow, crystalline ppt. Collect the ppt. and moisten it with conc. H_2SO_4: a play of colors as in § 435.

440. ANTIDOTES.—Stomach-pump; wash out stomach with infusion of tea. Chloroform, chloral.

TABLE OF SOLUBILITIES.

FRESENIUS.

W or w = soluble in H_2O. A or a = insoluble in H_2O; soluble in HCl, HNO_3, or aqua regia. I or i = insoluble in H_2O and acids. W-A = sparingly soluble in H_2O, but soluble in acids. W-I = sparingly soluble in H_2O and acids. A-I = insoluble in H_2O, sparingly soluble in acids. Capitals indicate common substances.

	Aluminium.	Ammonium.	Antimony.	Barium.	Bismuth.	Cadmium.	Calcium.	Chromium.	Cobalt.	Copper.	Ferrous.	Ferric.
Acetate	W	W		W	w	w	a	w	w	W	w	W
Arsenate	a	w	a	a	a	a	a	a	a	a	a	a
Arsenite		w	a	a			a		a	A	a	a
Benzoate	w	W		w		w	W			a	w	a
Borate	a	W		a	a	w-a	a	a	a	a	a	a
Bromid	w	W	w-a	w	w-a	w	w	w-i	W	W	w	w
Carbonate	a	W		A	A	a	A	a	A	A	A	a
Chlorate	w	w		W	w	w	w	w	w	w	w	W
Chlorid	w	W[2]	W-A[5]	W	W-A[10]	W	W	W-I	W	W	W	W
Chromate		w	a	a	a	a	w-a	a	a	w		w
Citrate	w	W		a			a	w-a	w	w	w	W
Cyanid		w		w-a			a	w	a	a-i	a	a-i	
Ferricyanid		w						w		i		I	w
Ferrocyanid		w		w-a				w		i	i	I
Fluorid	w	W	w	a-i	w	w-a	A	w	w-a	a	w-a	w
Formate	w	w		w	w	W	w	w	w	w	w	W
Hydrate	A	W	A	W	a	a	W-A	A	A	a	a	A
Iodid	w	W	w-a	w	a	W	w	w	w	w	W	w
Malate	w	w		w-a			w-a					W
Nitrate	w	W		W	W[11]	w	w	W	w	W	W	W
Oxalate	a	W	a	a	a	a	A	w-a	A	a	a	a
Oxid	A-I		a[7]	W	a	a	W-A	A-I	A	A	a	A
Phosphate	a	W[3]	w-a	w-a	a	a	W-A	a	a	a	a	a
Silicate	A-I			a		a	a	a	a	a	a	a
Succinate	w-a	w		w-a		w	w-a		w-a	w-a	w	
Sulfate	W[1]	W[4]	a	A	w	W	W-I	W-A[12]	W	W	W	W
Sulfid	a	W	A[8]	W	a	A	W-A	a i	a[13]	A	A	A
Tartrate	w	w[5]	a[9]	a	a	w-a	a	w	w	w	w-a	W[14]

[1] $(Al_2)(NH_4)_2(SO_4)_4$ = W; $(Al_2)K_2(SO_4)_4$ = W. [2] $As(NH_4)Cl_4$ = W; $Pt(NH_4)_2Cl_6$ = W-I. [3] $HNa(NH_4)PO_4$ = W; $Mg(NH_4)PO_4$ = A. [4] $Fe(NH_4)_2(SO_4)_2$ = W; $Cu(NH_4)_2(SO_4)_2$ = W. [5] $C_4H_4O_6K(NH_4)$ = W. [6] SbOCl = A. [7] Sb_2O_3 = soluble in HCl, not in HNO_3. [8] Sb_2S_3 = sol. in hot HCl, slightly in HNO_3. [9] $C_4H_4O_6K(SbO)$ = W. [10] BiOCl = A. [11] $(BiO)NO_3$ = A. [12] $(Cr_2)K_2(SO_4)_4$ = W. [13] CoS = easily sol. in HNO_3, very slowly in HCl. [14] $(C_4H_4O_6)_4(Fe_2)K_2$ = W.

TABLE OF SOLUBILITIES—Continued.

FRESENIUS.

W or w = soluble in H_2O. A or a = insoluble in H_2O; soluble in HCl, HNO_3, or aqua regia. I or i = insoluble in H_2O and acids. W-A = sparingly soluble in H_2O, but soluble in acids. W-I = sparingly soluble in H_2O and acids. A-I = insoluble in H_2O, sparingly soluble in acids. Capitals indicate common substances.

	Lead.	Magnesium.	Manganese.	Mercurous.	Mercuric.	Nickel.	Potassium.	Silver.	Sodium.	Strontium.	Stannous.	Stannic.	Zinc.
Acetate	W	w	w	w-a	w	w	W	w	W	w	w	w	W
Arsenate	a	a	a	a	a	a	W	a	W	a	a	a	..
Arsenite	a	a	a	a	a	a	W	a	W	a	a	..	..
Benzoate	a	w	w	a	w-a	..	w	w-a	w	..	..	..	..
Borate	a	w-a	a	..	..	a	W	a	W	a	a	..	a
Bromid	w-i	w	w	a-i	w	w	W	a	W	w	..	..	w
Carbonate	A	A	A	a	a	A	W	a	W	A	..	..	A
Chlorate	w	w	w	w	w	w	W	w	W	w	w	..	w
Chlorid	W-I	W	W	A-I	W[20]	W	W[26]	I	W	W	W	W	W
Chromate	A-I	w	w	a	w-a	a	W	a	w	w-a	a	..	w
Citrate	a	w	a	a	w-a	w	w	a	W	a	..	..	w-a
Cyanid	a	W	a	..	..	W	a-i	W	i	w	w	..	a
Ferricyanid	w-a	w	i	..	..	i	W	i	w	..	..	..	a
Ferrocyanid	a	w	a	..	..	i	W	i	w	w	..	..	a-i
Fluorid	a	a-i	a	..	w-a	w-a	w	w	w	a-i	w	w	w-a
Formate	w-a	w	w	w	w	w	w	w	W	w	w	..	w
Hydrate	a	A	A	a	..	a	W	..	W	w	a	a	a
Iodid	W-A	w	w	A	A	w	W	i	W	w	w	w	w
Malate	w-a	w	w	a	w-a	..	w	w-a	w	w	w	w	w
Nitrate	W	w	w	W	W	W	W	W	W	W	W	..	w
Oxalate	a	a	w-a	a	a	a	W	a	W	a	a	w	a
Oxid	A	A	A[15]	A	A	A	W	a	W	W	a	A-I	A
Phosphate	a	a[2]	a	a	a	a	w	a	W	a	a	a	a
Silicate	a	a	a	..	..	a	W	..	W	a	..	..	a
Succinate	a	w	w	w	w-a	w	w	a	w	w-a	..	a	w-a
Sulfate	A-I	W	W	w-a	W[17]	W	W[12]	W-A	W	I	w	..	W
Sulfid	A	a	a	a	A[18]	A[19]	W	a[21]	W	w	a[22]	A[22]	A[23]
Tartrate	a	w-a	w-a	w-a	a	a	W	a	w	a	a	..	a

[15] MnO_2 = sol. in HCl; insol. in HNO_3. [16] Mercurammonium chlorid = A. [17] Basic sulfate = A. [18] HgS = insol. in HCl and in HNO_3, sol in aq. regia. [19] See 13. [20] PtK_2Cl_6 = W-A. [21] Only soluble in HNO_3. [22] Sn sulfids = sol. in hot HCl; oxidized, not dissolved, by HNO_3. Sublimed $SnCl_4$ only sol. in aq. regia. [23] Easily sol. in HNO_3, difficultly in HCl.

Au_2S = insol. in HCl and in HNO_3, sol. in aq. regia. $AuBr_3$, $AuCl_3$, and $Au(CN)_3$ = w; AuI_3 = a. PtS_2 = insol. in HCl, slightly sol. in hot HNO_3; sol. in aq. regia. $PtBr_4$, $PtCl_4$, $Pt(CN)_4$, $Pt(NO_3)_4$, $(C_2O_4)_2Pt$, $Pt(SO_4)_2$ = w; PtO_2 = a; PtI_4 = i.

INDEX.

Abbreviations, 3
Acetates, 14
Acid, carbolic, 89
　　hydrochloric, 10
　　hydrocyanic, 87
　　meconic, 106
　　nitric, 13
　　prussic, 87
　　residues, 10, 21, 22
　　sulfuric, 15
　　uric, 50, 71, 75
Acidimetry, 62
Acids, 10, 21, 22, 90
Albumin, 50, 72
Alcohol, 87
Alkalies, 91
Alkalimetry, 62
Alkaloids, 104
Aluminium, 25
Ammonium, 29
Antimonates, 19
Antimonites, 19
Antimony, 99
Arsenates, 18
Arsenic, 94
Arsenites, 18

Barium, 30, 101
Bases, 22, 34, 35, 37
Bile, 59
Bismuth, 26, 100
Blood, 58
　　corpuscles, 79
Borates, 19
Bromids, 11
Bunsen burner, 5

Calcium, 29
　　oxalate, 76
Calculi, 82
Carbonates, 16
Casts, 80
Chloral, 88
Chlorates, 14
Chlorids, 10, 65
Chloroform, 88
Citrates, 20
Copper, 31, 101
Cyanids, 12
Cystin, 78.

Decantation, 6

Epithelium, 79

Ferric, 24
Ferrous, 24
Filtration, 6

Glucose, 54, 73

Hydroxids, 14

Iodids, 11
Iron, 24

Lead, 25, 101
Leucin, 77
Lithium, 27

Magnesium, 30
Manganese, 24

Manganic, 24
Manganous, 24
Measures, 4
Mercury, 32, 101
Morphin, 105
Mucin, 53
Mucous corpuscles, 78

Nitrates, 13

Oxalates, 17
Oxids, 14

Paraglobulin, 53
Peptone, 53
Phenol, 89
Phosphates, 18, 66, 77
Phosphorus, 85
Poisons, 84
   metallic, 91
   mineral, 90
   vegetable, 102
   volatile, 84
Potassium, 28
Precipitation, 8
Pus, 78

Reaction, 9, 47, 62
Reactions of acids, 10, 21, 22
   of bases, 22, 34, 35, 37
Rules, 1

Silver, 29
Sodium, 28
Solubility, table of, 108, 109
Solution, 6
Spermatozoa, 81
Stannic, 27
Stannous, 27
Strychnin, 106
Sugar, 54

Sulfates, 68
Sulfids, 14
Sulfites, 15

Tartrates, 17
Test, Boettger's, 55
   biuret, 50, 54
   Fehling's, 58, 73
   fermentation, 57
   Gmelin's, 61
   Heller's, 51
   Marsh's, 97, 100
   Moore's, 55
   Mulder-Neubauer, 56
   murexid, 50
   Oliver's, 60
   Pettenkofer's, 59
   Reinsch's, 96, 99
   Trommer's, 55
Thiosulfates, 16
Tin, 27
Tyrosin, 77

Urates, 76
Urea, 49, 69
Urinary deposits 75
Urine, color, 46
   composition, 49
   physical characters, 46
   odor, 46
   qualitative analysis, 46
   quantitative analysis, 62
   quantity, 46
   reaction, 47, 62
   specific gravity, 47

Weights, 4

Zinc, 31, 101

www.ingramcontent.com/pod-product-compliance
Lightning Source LLC
Chambersburg PA
CBHW031354160426
43196CB00007B/812